Parenting Wisdom

What To Teach The Children

Richard Andrew King

No part of this publication may be reproduced or transmitted in any form or by any means, electronic or mechanical, including photocopy, recording or any information storage and retrieval system now known or to be invented without permission in writing from the publisher, except by a reviewer who wishes to quote brief passages in connection with a review written for inclusion in a magazine, newspaper, online article or broadcast. Contact Richard King Publications, PO Box 3621, Laguna Hills, CA 92654.

This book and its information contain copyrighted material, trademarks and other proprietary information. You may not modify, publish, transmit, participate in the transfer or sale of, create derivative works of, or in any way exploit, in whole or in part, any Proprietary or other Material in any capacity in this work.

Library of Congress Cataloging-in-Publication Data
King, Richard Andrew
Parenting Wisdom – What To Teach The Children
ISBN: 978-0-931872-14-3
Date of Publication: 27 June 2013

© by Richard Andrew King
Published by Richard King Publications
PO Box 3621
Laguna Hills, CA 92654
(www.RichardKing.net)

Parenting Wisdom

What To Teach The Children

Richard Andrew King

ACKNOWLEDGMENT

With deep love, gratitude, and appreciation to my daughter Chandra King Lombard for her expert editorial work and loving support.

DEDICATION

To Commander, Hawkeye, Jaws, and Mavlock
for being exceptional and wonderful parents,
and to my beautiful grandchildren
Popeye, Pipes, and Lightning.

DISCLAIMER

This work is neither designed to extol or defame any person or entity. Its purpose is simply to share the author's personal parenting principles and guidelines in the hope of raising beautiful, substantive children.

Parenting Wisdom
What To Teach The Children

Table of Contents

Segment	Page
Author's Introduction	9
A Divine Reality	13
A Man's Worth Is Only Worth What His Word's Worth	17
Balance Is Primary	21
Be A Living Example	27
Better To Have A Gold Character Than A Gold Medal	31
Boundaries, Rules, And Regs	37
Competence Creates Confidence	47
Do The Right Thing Because It's The Right Thing To Do	53
Don't Dummy Down	57
Don't Rush In	61
First Comes Ticker	65
Give 'Em A Spine	69
Grown Ups, Own Up	75
High Bar, High Life; Low Bar, Low Life	79
How To Spoil A Child	89
It's Not All About Them	91
Living With Grace	97
Make It A Game	101
Managing Opposition	111

No Second Chance Guarantee	115
No Whining	119
Parental Sovereignty Of Children	121
Pity Pot Poison	125
Sticks And Stones	129
Tender Love Versus Tough Love	133
The Five Needs Of Children	139
The Four Cornerstones Of A Substantive Life	145
The Process Is The Product	151
The Temptations Of S.A.D.	155
The Two Sides Of Life	163
Where Have All The Manners Gone?	169
Your Life, Your Responsibility	175
You're On Your Own – Y.O.Y.O.	181
Quotations	187
Index	203

Author's Introduction

Parenting is a critical job, arguably the most important job in the world. Certainly one of the germane considerations and questions in parenting is what to teach the children.

Parenting is not an academic function. It's a common sense function. Anyone can be a good parent if they choose to be and are willing to make the tough decisions and sacrifices necessary.

Parenting is not a new concept. It is as old as mankind itself. However, this fast-moving, ever-changing new world often leaves new parents and parents-to-be in search of ideas which can assist them in raising their young.

Parenting Wisdom – What To Teach The Children addresses thirty-three universal, time-tested concepts and principles for raising healthy, whole, substantive children. This work is a companion book to *Parenting Wisdom For The 21st Century – Raising Your Children By Their Numbers To Achieve Their Highest Potential.* The former work focuses solely on concepts and principles; the latter addresses the numerological aspects of a child's destiny. They can be read separately and are not necessarily inclusive. However, for a full treatment of parenting wisdom, both works are recommended, especially in this 21st Century and for those parents who are forward-thinking.

The writing style I've chosen for this work is the most personal of my books to date. Within it I sometimes use the first person in order to share my direct thoughts and feelings, just as I would if I were teaching my own children, grandchildren, or students.

In *Parenting Wisdom* I express ideas about raising and guiding children which I have used successfully throughout my life. Put simply, I am here to share – to talk to you and put forth my ideas knowing full well that each parent has his or her own way of approaching parenting.

As raising and teaching children is an important function, here's a little background about me. I'm a father, grandfather, and professional martial arts instructor. I've taught thousands of people – children and adults alike – in my career, which began in the 1960s. I have a B.A. in English and a Standard Secondary Teaching Credential. I financed my way through college working with children in my city's Parks and Recreation Department. In my teenage years I had a booming babysitting business, and was ever grateful that parents were comfortable and confident in my ability to care for their children. The point I want to make is that my knowledge of parenting and teaching has not been cultivated from academic texts or coursework; it stems from a lifetime of direct experience with children.

Please note that sometimes I can be very direct and firm. I make no apologies for this. In fact, I believe the firm and direct approach is needed today more than ever. My professional martial arts teaching experience has given me many insights related to sculpting individuals in order to help them attain a high level of skill and personal conduct. In doing so, sometimes I had to be soft and gentle; sometimes tough and firm, even unrelenting. My goal has always been to create excellence in those children and adults who seek me out for the things I have to offer. I do not believe in mediocrity, hypersensitivity, political correctness, or enabling people's weaknesses. I believe in making people strong, courageous, confident, independent, whole, and substantive. This has and will always be what I regard as a sacred responsibility to those whom I serve, whether as a parent, grandparent, or teacher.

For the Love of Children,

Richard Andrew King

A Divine Reality

From my humble point of view the absolute first lesson to teach the children is that there is *A Divine Reality* to this creation. As Isaac Newton, regarded by many as the greatest scientist in history, stated:

> *In the absence of any other proof, the thumb alone would convince me of God's existence.*

Newton also proclaimed:

> *God created everything by number, weight, and measure.*

and . . .

> *It is the perfection of God's works that they are all done with the greatest simplicity. He is the God of order and not of confusion.*

Albert Einstein, arguably the greatest scientist of the 20th Century, said:

> *Everyone who is seriously involved in the pursuit of science becomes convinced that a spirit is manifest in the laws of the Universe - a spirit vastly superior to that of man, and one in the face of which we, with our modest powers, must feel humble.*

My personal experience and professional numerology work have proven to me beyond any shadow of any doubt that there is a power so incredibly vast it transcends the comprehension of the human mind. This power is real, it is alive, it is supremely intelligent, it is conscious, omnipotent, omniscient, and omnipresent. It is the center of everything, created everything, and sustains everything. It is the alpha and omega. It is, in fact, God.

The truth of this Divine Reality can easily be understood through numerology – the ancient art and science of numbers in which numbers are simply labels for energies defining and describing our lives and destinies.

Einstein's comment regarding individuals *seriously involved in the pursuit of science* becoming *convinced that a spirit is manifest in the laws of the universe* is corroborated through a serious study of numerology, by which it is impossible to negate, disclaim, denounce, or dismiss the reality of such a supernal Power. The intricacy and perfection between the events and conditions of people's lives in concert with the numbers and letters associated with their birth date and birth name irrefutably indicate an underlying power at work that is beyond man's comprehension and current awareness. (For those wishing to know more about numerology, especially as it applies to children, read the companion work to this book: *Parenting Wisdom For The 21st Century – Raising Your Children By Their Numbers To Achieve Their Highest Potential,* as well as other King's Numerology works.)

Knowing there is *A Divine Reality* to life should give any sentient person comfort and strength in at least two ways: 1) knowing there is an ultimate power in charge of everything; that life is not happenstance, and 2) that a relationship exists between the soul and its Source, i.e., God – a relationship beyond worldly relationships and one which can be developed if one chooses to pursue it.

No one is alone – on a worldly basis, perhaps, but not on a spiritual one. Each soul is a part of the divine whole just as a ray of light is to the sun or a drop of water is to the ocean.

The Gift of Life

None of us gave life to ourselves. In other words we did not create us. A higher power created us. Thus, each of our lives is a precious, priceless gift beyond measure. For children to understand this fact of life is also a great gift. So many people today either do not understand the divine reality of life, choose to ignore it, or disbelieve it. That's their choice. But those of us who do understand are in a perfect place to share this truth with our children, and should.

As humans, the greatest thing we can do for the gift of our lives is twofold: 1) *acknowledge* the gift and the Giver, and 2) *give thanks* for it. As we pursue the divine understanding of life and tread the spiritual path with its ultimate destination of union with God, our minds and hearts should be constantly effusing the simple phrase *Thank You, Thank You, Thank You*! Such exclamation of gratitude is important for children to adopt as an integral aspect of their consciousness. Regardless of one's spiritual or religious affiliation, one's centermost focus should be on gratitude to God.

Gratitude for one's life and its divine potential is privately manifest in three words: love, devotion, and purification – a triune expression of deep appreciation and action. When children internalize and inculcate this concept into their very beings, they will achieve a deeper connection between their soul and its Source, and their lives will be more integrated, full, whole, happy, and spiritually substantive with the potential of growing and expanding during the priceless gift of their priceless lives. There is nothing more powerful or critical we can do for our children than to make them aware of their intrinsic divine heritage and connection. (For more information on spirituality, read *Messages From the Masters – Timeless Truths For Spiritual Seekers* available through RichardKing.net and various retail outlets.)

Teaching Tips

1. First and foremost, teach children about their natural connection to God and the divine nature of their lives.

2. Instill in them a sense of acknowledgment and gratitude for their life and for that Divine Power that graced them with it. Give some time each day to privately expressing such gratitude – individually and as a family, either through thought, contemplation, meditation, or prayer.

3. Encourage children to pursue the connection of their soul with its Divine Source.

4. Teach them the power of *Thank You*.

A Man's Worth Is Only Worth What His Word's Worth

An individual may measure his value in many ways in this world. Among such measuring sticks are economic status, social connections, political power, athletic skill, educational degrees, technical abilities, celebrity popularity, movie stardom, championship trophies, awards and accolades from innumerable organizations, sexual attraction, beauty – the list is endless. Yet, arguably, the most important measure of a man is his word.

What is a man's *word*? A man's word is simply his undying ability to do what he says he will do, even at his own expense. A man's word is valuable because keeping one's word involves trust – the cornerstone of relationships. A man is simply not trustworthy if he doesn't do what he says he will do. We all naturally learn to trust people whose words match their actions. Such individuals have substantive worth whereas empty words have no worth at all.

A man's word is his bond. It is that link between his intentions and his actions. When a man keeps his word – again and again and again – he becomes trustworthy, i.e., worthy of trust, worthy, the root of which is *worth*.

If a man can't be counted upon to do what he says he will do, how can he be trusted? If he can't be trusted, what value does he have? Without a doubt, a man's worth is his value, and his value is based on him keeping his word.

Frankly, in this age where worth and value are determined by the externalities and superficialities of fame, fortune, status, beauty, celebrity, and sex appeal, it's challenging to find an individual who is good to his word. In truth, the sad fact of the world today is that it is extremely difficult to find a man who is good to his word, who has substantive and meaningful value. This is why *a man's worth is only worth what his word's worth.*

As children learn to keep their word, they will intrinsically develop a solid sense of self. We all know when we're doing wrong and when we're doing right. "Doing right" makes us whole. It integrates us. "Doing wrong" disintegrates us and makes us incomplete. When we are whole, we have value, and we know it. We, and our children, therefore move from step to step in life with confidence and a substantive sense of personal value that allows us to express our highest and best good and become worthy as human beings.

One of the main challenges people often have in keeping their word arises when money is involved. Unfortunately, money dirties one's hands as well as one's character. What some people do just for money is abominable. When a man who gives his word goes back on his word for any amount of money, his behavior is not only most untoward and ignoble, it renders him untrustworthy from that moment onward.

Therefore, we must teach our children to honor their word, to keep their promises and commitments and be cautious of selling themselves out for something as mundane as money. A man's character is worth more than gold, more than any precious metal or gem. A man's character cannot be bought. It is priceless. However, a man's character can be sold for whatever price he values as its worth.

The superior man will never sell his character for any amount of money.

> *We must not promise what we ought not, lest we be called on to perform what we cannot* (Abraham Lincoln).
>
> *Silver and gold are not the only coin; virtue too passes current all over the world* (Euripides, *Oedipus* - 4th Century B.C.).
>
> *God looks at the clean hands, not the full ones* (Publilius Syrus - *Moral Sayings* - 1st Century B.C.).

Teaching Tips

1. Be the living example of the truth you teach as a parent. We must keep our word if we expect our children to keep their word. Nothing kills faster than hypocrisy.

2. Constantly monitor your children's behavior to ensure their actions do equal their words. If they don't, explain to them they must learn to honor their life by making their actions equal their words.

3. Make sure that when your children make a promise they keep it. As soon as they learn to break a promise, they risk forming a habit of not keeping their word. When they don't keep their

word, people learn not to trust them. When their trust is gone, their value, their inner worth is gone.

Balance Is Primary

Balance is one of the most critical principles of living a meaningful, substantive, and happy life. There are many types of balance – physical, emotional, mental, spiritual, financial, sexual, and dietary, to name a few.

Think of a man walking across a tightrope a thousand feet in the air. His concentration must be perfect. His balance must be perfect. If he were to lose his balance he could well fall to his death.

How does the tightrope walker keep his balance? He does so by focusing on the *alignment* between his head, shoulders, hips, knees, feet, and the wire itself. This is what balance is – an alignment issue. If the factors contributing to the tightrope walker's balance are disarranged and out of sync, his position on the wire becomes compromised, dangerously placing his very life in peril.

Life is very much like a tightrope walking experience. It requires concentration and balance from birth to death to avoid missteps which could create mishaps leading to a lifetime of problems, or worse. This is one reason why Dariya of Bihar, the tailor Saint, stated:

You must tread your path with caution in the world.

Following this explanation, we would be wise to teach our children to be ever focused and centered on leading a balanced life. And how do they do this? Our children create a balanced life by keeping all aspects of themselves in the proper alignment – their physical self, emotional self, mental self, and as they mature, their sexual self, financial self, spiritual self, and intellectual self. No matter how many components of the "self" there are, they must all be kept in alignment to create the balance which would, in turn, generate a meaningful life.

As Pope John Paul II stated:

> *Man always travels along precipices. His truest obligation is to keep his balance.*

The ancient Greek playwright Euripides noted:

> *The best and safest thing is to keep a balance in your life, acknowledge the great powers around us and in us. If you can do that and live that way, you are really a wise man.*

And an anonymous observation:

> *Anyone can teeter-totter but not everyone can balance.*

This fundamental principle of balance is clearly understandable when we think of the fulcrum of a teeter-totter and how a person's balance is maintained by positioning himself at the centerpoint of the teeter-totter. This concept of balance is also the substance of Aristotle's *Golden Mean* (the desirable midpoint between two extremes) and the Confucian *Doctrine of the Mean*, as well as the Chinese Tao, which is represented by the Yin/Yang symbol. Unquestionably, the concept of balance is a potent universal principle for living a meaningful life.

Arguably, this brings us to the conclusion that one of the greatest and most fundamental life skills is balance. With it, life is potentially harmonious, productive, meaningful. Without it, life is extremely challenging, bringing a torrent of angst, confusion, destruction, non-productivity, and unhappiness. When the teeter-totter is constantly going up and down, how can stability be maintained? It can't, and where there is no stability, there is, axiomatically, instability and all of its attending problems, perils, issues, and evils.

It is not easy to achieve balance. Try standing on one leg for any length of time. It's difficult. Stand on an inflated rubber dome, disk, or gymnastics balance beam and the task becomes even more difficult. Still need more challenge? Try these balance exercises with your eyes closed. As time in the balance position increases, the challenge becomes practically overwhelming, resulting in falling off the mark. If standing on one foot is not challenging enough, try a handstand on the ground. Then proceed to parallel bars, gymnastic rings, or the balance beam again. Hardly easy skills. Even the best gymnast cannot hold his balance point for more than a few minutes on any given apparatus.

It is through these exercises that we understand balance is a dynamic and active process, not a passive one. Our mind, muscles, tendons, ligaments, and joints are all continually moving to keep us centered. We learn from such exercises that balance is truly a difficult state to maintain, not just in a physical sense, but also in a mental, emotional, and spiritual sense. Thus, leading a successful life becomes a continual struggle and is definitely not a passive activity but an energetic and constantly dynamic one.

Perhaps the most important ingredient of balance is concentration – a focus of our attention on the alignments that keep all of our body parts in sync in the physical realm. When standing on one foot, for example, the key to balance is to insure that our head, shoulders, hips, supporting knee, ankle, foot, and our body's center line are properly aligned, just like the tightrope walker. Thus, balance becomes a problem of alignment, as we've stated.

It is no different when we are working to keep our life in balance except that we have to expand our focus to include our mind, heart, spirit, health, finances, relationships, etc. – all aspects that are necessary to life. If properly aligned, they will insure a successful life through the principle of balance. Once we lose our focus, our alignment goes, and so goes our balance and with it the peace potentially generated from equanimity.

It is difficult to maintain balance in this world because it is based on a bipolar structure – the interplay of opposites. The ancient Yin/Yang symbol of the Chinese Tao beautifully depicts this ebb and flow of opposite energies: positive/negative, light/dark, male/female, hard/soft, day/night, up/down, hot/cold, happy/sad, good/bad, and so forth. In this world the great cosmic pendulum is forever swinging back and forth from one polarity to the other, and in such a constantly changing environment it is difficult to maintain balance. This is why mystics call this earth the "plane of struggle," and why our children are best served when we parents instruct them in the principle of balance.

Teaching Tips

1. Playing balance games with children is a great way to begin inculcating the concept of balance without being overly tutorial. For example, you might say in a fun manner, "Let's play a game and see how long we can stand on one leg?" And then you join them in the game. It makes it more fun when parents do things with their kids. While you're balancing, keep track of the time individually for you and each child. If a minute of balancing time on one leg is not reached, then you say, "Let's see if we can stand on one leg for a minute?" The idea, of course, is to keep extending the balance time, alternating between each leg. When the child meets a goal of one minute, or whatever the goal is, make sure you give positive feedback by congratulating the child, cheering, or applauding. This will reinforce to the child that being successful in balancing brings applause and recognition. All we're trying to do, whether the child knows it or not, is establish, either consciously or subconsciously, the reality that balance is critical to success. As the child matures, you can be more intellectually instructive, expanding the concept of balance to keeping one's emotions in tact and not getting too upset over things, managing homework versus play time, household chores versus visiting with friends, saving money *here* so you can spend it *there*, and so forth. The whole purpose of this training is to teach our children to stay centered and balanced so they don't fall off the beam of life and create unnecessary problems for themselves.

2. As children grow and mature, talk to them directly about the concept of balance and how important it is to their overall well-being.

3. If you give your children an allowance, help them learn to save and spend efficiently. And don't bail them out if they spend their money and then want something else they can't pay for. Let them earn their own money so they learn the value of a buck. If they're in discomfort because they can't have what they want because they spent all of their allowance, well, that's just too bad. Let 'em suffer a little bit. It's not life and death. Then next time they want something, they'll be more thoughtful about how they spend their money. Bailing them out every time they need help will not teach them how to manage (and balance) their lives efficiently. Our job as parents is to teach them to stand on their own two feet, not constantly indulge their every wish and whim. When we constantly indulge them and bail them out, we're actually crippling them, and that's not loving them. Love is teaching them to be independent and to manage their own lives effectively because, the fact remains, this is their life and it is their responsibility.

Be A Living Example

If we are going to be effective and successful parents and create in our children a strong foundation for their lives, we need to teach them by being a *living example* of our words – to this end we may not need words at all.

One of the greatest human beings of the 19th and 20th Centuries was German born Albert Schweitzer (1875 – 1965). This outstanding individual was a medical doctor, theologian, world class musician, philosopher, and extraordinary humanitarian. He received the Nobel Peace prize in 1952 for his philosophy, *Reverence for Life*.

Regarding the principle of *leading by example*, Dr. Schweitzer said:

> *Example is not the main thing in influencing others. It is the only thing.*

What more need be said? Example, example, example – this is what we need to be to create a model for our children and their futures. It does no good to tell our children one thing and do another. Such hypocrisy will be counter-productive and ultimately fail.

There was a time when it was common for parents to say, "Don't do as I do, do as I say," as if this were an acceptable child-rearing technique. It is not. It is a technique infused with failure, and it will be of no positive service to those sweet souls whom we brought into the world. Parenting is not a pastime. It is a vital responsibility, and one which must not be placed in a secondary position. As parents, our children come first, always.

"But I'm not perfect," a parent may say. This is true. None of us is perfect, but that should not exempt us from striving to be the best we can be as parents. If our actions match our intentions, that is what our children will gain. If we make mistakes, as we most likely will, we should do our best to fix them, improve ourselves, and move on. That's life.

However, if we mess up and excuse our failings without attempting to fix them, then our children will learn to do the same because that is the example we set for them. If we want the highest and best good for our children, we must do all we can to exude the highest and best in ourselves. After all, who else is there in the life of a little child to create an example of goodness? If it is not us, then who? As Saint Charan Singh states:

Children always copy their parents.

Our children deserve our best effort. We brought them into this world, and therefore our responsibility is to give them the best chance for a decent life that we can, and that chance is based on us being a *living example* for them.

Teaching Tips

1. As parents, we need to continually monitor our own behavior and make the changes in ourselves that are necessary to lead our children by example.

2. Support this *living example* strategy by pointing out to children other parents, adults, athletes, teachers, etc., who are leading by example. If we fail in being the *living example* for our children, then the next best thing is to draw upon those people who are living examples for others. This may take some humility on our part, but it will serve our children's best interest, which is certainly the main focus of effective, loving, and wise parenting.

Better To Have A Gold Character Than A Gold Medal

What do we aspire to in life? To what do we teach our children to aspire? By what standards do we teach our children to measure their achievement and success? Is it money? Fame? Name? Properties? Lands? Wealth? Celebrity? University degrees? Trophies? Gold medals?

All of the aforementioned symbols of achievement are universal. Yet, when we die they all die with us. None go with us into the next phase of our existence. They are all confined to this life, to this world.

On the contrary, what will go with us as our soul moves onward in its journey is our character because it is a function of the energy that *is* us. Our character is woven into the very fabric of who we are and what our soul is. Unlike the worldly items mentioned in the opening paragraph, our character is the only substantive aspect of our life that has lasting merit. Everything else is simply window dressing.

Furthermore, character cannot be bought for any amount of money. Worldly things all carry a worldly price tag. Fame can be bought. University degrees are costly. Trophies and gold medals can be earned, but history has proven that they are not always achieved honestly nor honorably. The only thing we have of any true and lasting merit is our character and its quality. Regarding a spiritual life, Saint Sawan Singh states:

> *The first essential step to a spiritual life is character. One may deceive one's friends, relatives, and even oneself but the Power within is not deceived.*

Eleanor Roosevelt, wife to United States President Franklin Delano Roosevelt, quite beautifully and succinctly remarked:

> *Only a man's character is the real criterion of worth.*

Character is based on virtue – the amalgam of our moral and ethical principles, both of which are developed through the process of living, not the process of buying or conniving. It is axiomatic that the higher our morals and ethics are, the higher our character becomes.

Following is a sampling of quotations on virtue from famous individuals.

> *Recommend to your children virtue; that alone can make them happy, not gold* (Beethoven).

> *There was never yet a truly great man that was not at the same time truly virtuous* (Benjamin Franklin).

> *Silver and gold are not the only coin; virtue too passes current all over the world* (Euripides).

> *Of all the fragrances . . . the fragrance of virtue is the sweetest* (Buddha).

> *The superior man thinks always of virtue; the common man thinks of comfort* (Confucius).

> *Few men have virtue to withstand the highest bidder* (George Washington).

> *The only reward of virtue is virtue* (Ralph Waldo Emerson).

> *Glory follows virtue as if it were its shadow* (Cicero).

Perhaps one of the most powerful aspects of character is that it must be developed, honed, and sharpened through self-reflection, examination, analysis, effort, resolve, conscious transformation, and determination. This should give comfort to those individuals who have never been acknowledged for being successful in this world. Although seldom recognized, character is the greatest mark of life achievement and should garner the highest praise and applause.

Helen Keller is one of the most famous icons in world history, a true testament to personal character. Her thoughts are quite germane.

> *Character cannot be developed in ease and quiet. Only through experience of trial and suffering can the soul be strengthened, ambition inspired, and success achieved.*

What Keller is saying, of course, is that character development takes work and effort. It is also neither a function of an easy nor peaceful life. Rather, character is created through the fires of life, fires allowing us the opportunity to sculpt, sharpen, and define the energetic fibers of our virtue. Saint Charan Singh says:

> *The first prerequisite of a gentleman or a lady is a good moral character.*

The bottom line is that if we want our children to have great character, we would be wise to teach them that the lumps and bumps that will surely occur in their lives, as they occur in all our lives, have great silver linings and blessings even though they may be uncomfortable at the time. Such lumps and bumps give us great opportunities for developing character, the most priceless of gems. By using this strategy we prepare our children for the realities of life. We help them become aware, balanced, strong, and whole.

Gold medals or a gold character – which would you prefer your children to have? Gold medals have a price. A gold character is priceless. Gold medals gain us nothing but temporary recognition. A gold character infuses our being with spiritually enduring energy.

Teaching Tips

1. Always reinforce the idea that character is the highest reflection of a successful life and a great person. It trumps everything else. Without a solid character how can there be any solid or substantive achievement?

2. Play down the view that success is solely based on money, wealth, name, fame, celebrity, etc. There is nothing wrong with

these success markers as long as they are placed in a subservient position to personal character. Character first, everything else follows.

3. If children ever feel dismayed or upset because other people do not recognize the value of character, remind them that worldly people only love worldly things, and that success and achievement based only on worldly criteria are deficient, which they are by all spiritual teachings.

4. Repetition is a great learning tool. If children grow knowing that their character is the supreme standard for judging success, and they are rooted in this thought, their lives will be more meaningful, substantial, happy, whole, and well-adjusted.

Boundaries, Rules, And Regs

Kids need boundaries. They need rules to live by and regulations to follow. Children are neither mature enough, old enough, experienced enough, or wise enough to know what is good for them. That's why there are parents. It is our job to establish restrictive lines of behavior which will protect our children from conduct and actions that could jeopardize their ability to live a full, whole, meaningful, substantive, and harmonious life.

In the thousands of children I've personally taught in my professional life as a martial arts instructor, I've never seen a child make the difficult but wise choice when confronted with an easier choice. Children need guidance, and if we adults don't give it to them, where will they get it, if they get it at all?

When I was in graduate school working for my Secondary Teaching Credential, I did a paper on self-esteem in children. The findings were that children who grew up with rules and boundaries had a much higher self esteem level than those who grew up with few to no boundaries. This knowledge was instrumental in my own development as both a teacher and father.

Think of a garden. If it is left unattended it will soon become a jungle of weeds, sprawling vines, ragged bushes. Basically, a mess. And if the vines or bushes have thorns, ouch! Kids are like gardens. If they're allowed to grow without boundaries, rules, or regulations they will become wild, unruly, undisciplined, and out-of-control. Such behavior is a disaster in the making.

In this metaphor, however, there is a key difference between growing children and growing gardens: gardens will never have the ability to self-regulate while children can. Gardens cannot prune themselves. Left to their own devices they will grow ragged, or even perish. Children, however, who have been blessed with parents who impose restrictions, create rules, follow regulations – in essence, provide boundaries – will have a model for setting their own internal restrictions as they mature into adulthood. They will learn to set and abide by their own boundaries.

Kids love boundaries, and they need them. They may rebel against them, but they're just testing their own limits. It's normal. As a parent and teacher, I've never had a child not test me. Kids begin testing right out of the womb. They want to see where the boundaries are and who the boss is. Unfortunately, many parents do not understand this, and subsequently they do not take charge and exhibit the level of leadership needed to guide and shape their children well.

Parents taking charge of their young is the natural order of life. Have you ever watched a mare with her foals? A mare is very tender with her young, but if her babies get out of hand and overstep their boundaries, their mother will directly set them straight. Mares can be very tough moms if need be. Horses understand rules. They're herd animals, and there are rules the herd lives by. In fact, what animal species doesn't have a system of rules, regulations, and boundaries for their young, and for their societies?

It's the same with humans. We live in herds but we call them families. Same thing. When the rearing of our young takes center stage we need to set the rules and enforce them. It's the natural order of life.

One of the problems, however, is that parents don't often set boundaries, rules, or regulations, and they let their children do what they want to do. The result is that the children grow up with no sense of structure, discipline, restriction, or self-control. Then when confronted with the rules or regulations imposed by a job, school, community, organization, or society, they often have problems adjusting, making success harder to achieve. Uncontrolled lives create all kinds of problems and self-defeating behaviors.

Order is a natural part of life. Order comes from rules and boundaries. Without order, there is chaos. Unrestricted lives are dangerous lives. A wise man will learn to establish his own internal restrictions to prevent the problems caused from his unrestricted actions and behaviors.

First and foremost, we parents need to remember that we are the parents. This may seem obvious, but there are those parents who believe their children are wiser than they are wise. Such parents often let their children make decisions which they (the children) should not be making. In doing so, such parents willingly abdicate their responsibility to set the framework for the familial structure and their child's future decision-making processes.

Heeding my parenting and instructor responsibilities, I employed one basic philosophy with my children and students: *I'm the boss and you're not*. This standard set the stage, the boundaries, and the environment of the parent/child, teacher/student relationship. Having established this reference point, I then needed to make sure I made decisions that would benefit those to whom I was responsible, decisions that would ensure their highest and best chances of success, whether they realized it or not. I was tough but fair and consistent.

The point is, someone has to be the boss, to make tough decisions, hopefully wise decisions, to lead, to go first, to be responsible. If there is no leader, there will be problems and subsequent chaos.

Parents, first and foremost, must be the boss, not the children, and this aspect should be made clear and decisive from the get-go so there is no confusion in the parent/child relationship. Being the "boss" may be difficult for some parents who are not naturally disposed to being a leader. Yet, making the decision to have children carries with it an intrinsic and irrefutable condition and responsibility of leadership. Parents lead, children follow. When children become parents, they will be the leaders of their children and their families. Such is the circle and cycle of life.

In setting boundaries, rules, and regulations there must always be a line between what is allowed and what is not, what is acceptable and what is not acceptable. It doesn't have to be a harsh, unbending line, but there must be a line. Children must know what the consequences will be if they cross that line. That has to be set by the parents. Furthermore, the same rules must apply to all the children in the family. If not, favoritism will set in, and that will create problems, not to mention the potential negative effects it will have on the child or children who are on the negative end.

When establishing boundaries it is wise to explain the purpose of such boundaries when the children are capable of understanding. Explaining dangers of certain actions, as well as problems and unnecessary challenges that could result if lines were crossed and not respected, is important for the development of wisdom in the growing child.

After all, the foundation set as a result of the boundaries, rules, and regulations established in the formative years will be the structure on which the child's entire life will be lived. Once the trunk of the tree is rooted and set, the base cannot be changed. The tree will grow from its base and root structure. If we give our children a strong foundation, their chances of having a balanced and substantive life are highly increased.

I have other rules and guidelines in my parenting/teaching tool kit. Following is a brief list of twenty-five in random order . . .

1. If you make a mess, you clean it up. It's not my, your mother's or anyone else's job to clean up your mess. It's your mess and it's your responsibility to clean it up. Why? Because *It's your life, it's your responsibility.*

2. No whining. It's unbecoming. It weakens your character. Everyone has their tales of woe to tell. There's no need to tell yours.

3. If you give your word, you keep it. If you don't think you can keep your word, then don't give it. A person is only worth what his word's worth. Anyone can walk the walk or talk the talk. You make sure you walk your talk.

4. Tell the truth, even if it hurts.

5. Do your best in school. That's your job. I don't care what grade you get as long as you give 100% of what you can give.

Giving less than 100% is not acceptable. When you give less than you can, you're cheating yourself and betraying your full potential. That's not allowed. Be true to your highest potential. There can be no excellence without effort.

6. Be kind to others. Be respectful. Have a good, kind, and tender heart.

7. Character is critical to being a substantive individual. Without character, what else is left? Character must precede prowess.

8. Show respect to adults. Address them as Mr., Mrs., Miss, or Ms.

9. If you start something, you finish it. Be the first to begin and the last to clean up.

10. Lead by example. It is the only true way to lead.

11. Don't allow mistakes to cripple you. When you make a mistake, fix it and move on. That's life. Wallowing in the past will weigh you down and keep you from moving forward.

12. There's no disgrace in falling down. The disgrace is in not getting back up. Failure is part of the success process. Never be afraid to fail. The road to success is paved with failure.

13. Challenge your fears. Don't let them detain or defeat you. You defeat them.

14. Look to the consequences of your actions *before* you make them. Life doesn't always give second chances.

15. Be prepared. Preparation is the key to success. If you fail to prepare, you prepare to fail.

16. Stand up for yourself. If you don't, who will?

17. If you're wrong, apologize. Owning up to your mistakes shows strength, not weakness.

18. What are the magic words? (*Please* and *Thank You*).

19. Be grateful. Remember, no one has to do anything for you, and if they do something for you, it's inappropriate not to thank them, even in the smallest of actions, such as opening a door.

20. Set your priorities. Do the most important things first. My suggestion: family chores and duties come first, schoolwork second, developmental actives third (such as music lessons, martial arts, sports, etc.), and playtime last.

21. Be gracious in victory and in defeat. Don't be a cry baby. Congratulate your opponents. Giving grace is a class act and the sign of a true champion.

22. Always remember, humility is the highest form of strength; arrogance is the highest form of weakness.

23. Stay balanced in all aspects of your life. Balance is primary.

24. Concentration is the first key.

25. Have courage and be strong. Strength is the ability to endure.

Teaching Tips

1. Boundaries, rules, and regulations must be established to ensure a solid foundation for children as they grow and to help them achieve a high level of self-esteem. Tell them, "You may do this, but you may not do that," or "This is acceptable but that is not." The key is to make known those behaviors that will result in some form of disciplinary or corrective action if violated. By setting boundaries, parents also establish that they're the boss, the leader, the one in charge.

2. Boundary lines must be reasonable, firm, and fair.

3. Be consistent when enforcing boundaries. Being inconsistent just shows children you're not serious, which can confuse children, not to mention opening the door to parental challenge and manipulation.

4. As children mature, boundary lines may be adjusted with the maturity level of the children. In effect, that's what we want as parents – to create wisdom in our children so they can manage their own lives successfully. As parents, it is not, nor should be, our job to manage our children's lives for the entirety of their lives. Their lives are their responsibilities. If we do our job raising them, this will never be an issue, let alone a problem. If we do not do our job well, we may well regret it later, as might our children.

Competence Creates Confidence

Do you want to create confidence in your children, true confidence? Then there is only one way to do that. Teach them to be competent. Kissing children on the cheek, patting them on the head, embracing them with warm hugs, showering them with praise and the enduring phrase "I love you" may make them feel loved, secure, and nurtured, but it will not make them confident. In fact, it may give them a fatal sense of delusion. Creating true confidence begins with three simple words – *competence creates confidence*.

One of the greatest blessings of my destiny has been to be honored with the profession of being a martial arts instructor. Martial arts is life. There is nothing in martial arts training that does not in some way apply to life and its many lessons and challenges, especially in the creation of confidence. Unquestionably, the most vaunted personal attribute acquired through martial arts training is confidence. This has been told to me time and time again by students and parents alike. When asked what the most valuable attribute martial arts training has given to them or their children, the number one answer – confidence.

And how is confidence created? Confidence is simply created by making people competent in four ways: 1) by giving them accurate knowledge and skills; 2) teaching them how to use such information; 3) inspiring in them a sense of their own courage, strength, power, determination, goodness, worth, and character; 4) placing them in the "fire" to coalesce these ingredients into a fierce amalgam of undeniable personal capability. That amalgam of capability manifests as confidence, and it is beautiful. There is nothing greater, especially for me as a teacher/instructor/father/grandfather, than to see an individual blossom into a radiant, competent, and confident flower.

Is this an easy process? No. It is difficult and challenging, but what alternative is there? Do we want our children to grow up as insecure, frightened, hesitant, vacillating, incompetent, unsuccessful adults who, then, may well be incapable of raising their own children successfully? Of course we don't. As concerned parents, we want the best for our children, which means we must do all we can to make our children competent – not just in some educational, athletic, social, or artistic endeavor, but as people. Confidence resides at the core of a person's being, not in the extremities of his or her external activities.

Arguably, the most challenging aspect of creating confidence in anyone is to place them in the fire, so to speak, or at least refrain from rescuing them from problematic situations they will undoubtedly encounter in life. The fires of life are those situations which create problems for us to solve, be they personal, social, academic, athletic, recreational, financial, and so forth.

All of us, including our children, must learn to manage our own problems and solve them. Having people continually rescue us or solve our problems for us will not create confidence in us because it was someone else's competence that solved the problem rather than our own competence. We only gain confidence when *we* solve the problems of life through our own competence. The same is true for our children. They may have to endure some heat, bumps, bruises, and failures in the process, but that is the way they ultimately learn, succeed, and gain confidence – by do things for themselves.

This does not mean we should totally abandon our children when help is critical to their well-being. Of course we should help. However, as I've always taught my children, grandchildren, and students:

> *Diamonds are made under extreme heat and pressure over an extended period of time; not by a mere and casual blowing of an intermittent wind.*

Therefore, if we want our children to have confidence, we must allow them to manage the heat, pressure, and time necessary to create in them a diamond-like spirit, which in turn will create the competence underlying their confidence.

Teaching Tips

1. Never criticize, ridicule, denigrate, or in any way degrade or belittle your children. Use positive reinforcement. Compliment them on the things they do well, while encouraging them to do better. We cannot sculpt an enduring and beautiful image if we are continually tearing it down or marring it. You can give a child a thousand compliments and one negatively destructive remark, and the thing the child will most likely remember is that one destructive blow. This does not mean to neglect discipline or positive criticism, but these should be executed with love and understanding.

2. Do not give false praise. It only creates delusionary self-images and weakens the child in the long run. Do, however, give positive praise when deserved, but be careful in giving too much praise. In giving too much praise children run the risk of becoming too full of themselves, which can lead to egocentricity, arrogance, a loss of humility, a sense of entitlement, loss of respect among their peers, and other problematic issues. As all things in life, praise must be given judiciously. Too much of anything, even life-giving water, can be lethal.

3. Do not praise or applaud negative, rude, obnoxious, disrespectful, inconsiderate, arrogant, or reprehensible conduct. This only gives children a green light and sends them the wrong message, which in the long run will not serve their best interests. Teach humility. Explain to them that taking the high road but the low ground is always the best formula for success.

4. Don't do everything for your children. This will only cripple them. They must learn to do for themselves, to stand on their own two feet. If they don't learn to do for themselves, how can they be confident? They will naturally lack the competence so needed to create the confidence that makes them whole.

5. When children are confronted with a challenge, unless life-threatening, don't rush to their aid. Let them try to figure it out on their own. When they do, congratulate them, complimenting them on their ability to solve their own problems. Now is the time for kisses, hugs, and embraces because such actions will

strongly reinforce the child's ability to face, engage, and solve problems by himself or herself. Ultimately, their life is their life, and they must learn how to manage it successfully, the earlier the better. If we're constantly protecting them and doing for them those things they are capable of doing for themselves, we cripple them by disabling their intrinsic initiative, strength, courage, self-reliance, determination, resourcefulness, resolve, will, and independence. As parents, we must be true lovers and leaders, not enablers.

Do the Right Thing Because It's the Right Thing to Do

What do I do? This question is one which will confront every human being on the face of the earth multiple times during his or her lifetime when presented with a choice, especially a critical choice – one that involves our character, self-worth, dignity, and nobility. As surely as the sun rises and sets, the question, "What do I do?" will definitely challenge our children as they grow to adulthood. Is there a basic and sound response to this question? Actually, yes.

When confronted with a choice or choices of what to do in a particular situation, the answer is simply this: *Do the right thing because it's the right thing to do*. This obviously begs the question, "What is the right thing?" The simple truth is that each of us intrinsically knows what the right thing to do is. The problem is that we weigh the "right" thing to do with our desires, needs, and wants, which may be in conflict with what we know to be the correct course of action. It is the friction and confrontation created by our internal awareness of what is right versus our human desires that is the problem.

It takes courage to do the right thing. It also takes honesty, a developed sense of ethics and morality, and the ability to say 'no' to whatever mundane desires, needs, or wants are standing in the way of us making the correct choice, the ethical choice, the higher choice. If our worldly desires trump our ethics, we will forego the ethical choice in favor of the self-serving desire – be that "self-serving desire" money, fame, fortune, celebrity, social acceptance, a job, and so forth.

Within each of us there is a still, small voice that knows what to do, a voice that is connected to the divine energy of life itself. In reality, when we ask a question, we already know the answer. We sometimes wrestle with it because of our desires and what we may lose in the process of making the right choice, but the answer is always – *we should do the right thing because doing the right thing is the right thing to do.*

However, oftentimes we do the wrong thing, not the right thing. In doing so we sacrifice our noble potential, acquiring instead the ignoble robes of personal gratification. Yet, if we want to lead a substantive life of value, dignity, honor, and decency, we must learn to do the right thing, whatever the cost to ourselves. This is one of the great tests of life. If we pass it, we will move up the ladder of consciousness and spirituality. If we fail it, we can rest assured we will continue to be tested and challenged until we get it right. Therefore, the sooner we get "it" right the better.

Perhaps the operative question (in multiple forms) we should be asking ourselves when confronted with doing the right thing is, "What is our dignity worth? Our nobility? Our character? Our soul?" Are any of these precious aspects of *us* worth us not doing the right thing? Each individual will have to answer for himself.

A couple things must be kept in mind if one has trouble doing the right thing. First, what we place onto the circle of life will, by natural law, circle back to encircle us. In other words, what we do will be done to us. If we do good things, we can expect good things to eventually come back to us. If we do negative, destructive, evil things, then we will experience the same thing sooner or later. There is no avoiding this truth. What we sow we reap, and we cannot reap what we do not sow. This is an irrefutable law of this universe, in spite of its disacknowledgment by many in the masses.

Second, if we have a conscience, will we be able to rest peacefully at night knowing that we did not do the right thing? Will the negative aspects of our ill-doing haunt us mercilessly? What will the pain, suffering, sorrow, regret, and disturbance of making the wrong choice be when we know it is the wrong choice? Are we willing to pay such a price? Are we willing to live with regret?

One strategy to use when having to make a choice is simply to ask yourself the question, "Is this the right thing to do?" Then be quiet and listen to your conscience. It will tell you exactly what you should do if you listen carefully. Sometimes that *still, small voice* is neither still nor small. From my personal experience it has never been wrong. If you use it, I believe you will find it will never lead you astray.

This developmental skill, which I call *internal listening*, will yield great benefits. It just needs attention and practice. For example, how many times in your life has this *still, small voice* directed you to do something which you ignored, only to discover after the fact that it was right? I believe this ability to *listen internally* is a lost sense, a skill which is just as important, if not more important, than our normal five senses. It can be learned and perfected. We just have to be aware of its presence and power. Honing such a skill would certainly be a worthy item to place on anyone's "to do" list.

Teaching Tips

1. No doubt your children will be confronted with having to make the "right" choice at some time in their life. Use this opportunity to discuss personal worth, dignity, nobility, and character. What will the cost and consequences be if the wrong choice is made? What will the benefits be if the right choice is made? Remember, the easy choice is what most people settle for, especially children. However, it may not be the best choice. Doing the right thing is always the best choice because it's the right thing to do.

2. Discuss the concept of the "still small voice within" with your children. Ask them if they've ever experienced it. If they have, encourage them to develop it. If they have not, make them aware of it and suggest they "listen" more deeply in the future. Eventually, mastering this lost art will yield great benefits.

3. If you ever see your child making the "wrong" choice, ask them if such a choice is the right thing to do. This will let them know their choice may not have been correct and they should correct it if possible or make better choices in the future. Don't scold, criticize, or chastise them. Guide them. Lead them. Show them the way.

Don't Dummy Down

One of the most important principles we parents can follow is to never dummy-down our children, dummy-down their dreams, or dummy-down the expectations we have set for them. How can our children ever express a high level of self-confidence, self-esteem, or success in life if they are made to feel less than they are, or to be less than all they can be? As you continue reading, you may well feel a sense of "dummy down" overkill, but this is one of those subjects about which I am deeply passionate, and if being redundant gets the point across, then so be it.

As individuals and parents, we may not have achieved a high level of self-confidence, life success, or fulfillment of our dreams and aspirations, but we should not allow such conditions to negatively affect our children. Quite the contrary. As loving parents, it is our sacred obligation to do all we can to help our children and ensure their well-being, wholeness, self-confidence, success, and the fulfillment of their dreams.

This can be a challenge in today's world because there exists a very obvious trend in our society to dummy-down everything and everyone. The world continues to degrade at a rapid rate, as noted by the denigration of qualities such as success, virtue, wholesomeness, exceptionalism, character, and purity of conduct.

Why? Why dummy-down such venerable and inveterate life qualities? How can dummying down our children or their dreams and aspirations possibly build them up? Obviously, it can't. So why do it?

If we want our children to have the best lives possible, we must do everything in our power to set high standards and expectations for them and follow through from their birth until they are emancipated, which is usually around age eighteen – the normally accepted entrance into adulthood.

In setting high standards for our kids, we must not fall into the trap of believing that just because other people are dummying down their lives that we have to dummy-down our lives, as well as the expectations we have set for our own children.

Even if the whole world were to preach, teach, promote, and support a dummy-down philosophy and lifestyle, we must not. Just because the masses believe one way, does not mean we have to go along to get along, especially if "going along" leads us right into the abyss. To go along with a dummy-down mindset makes us dummies, subjecting us and our offspring to all of its undesirable consequences.

As far as the dummying down of life is concerned, it's best not to go along at all with such a limiting philosophy but remain steadfast in preaching, teaching, promoting, and supporting the upward course of striving for excellence in both life and conduct. Rare? Yes, but absolutely obligatory if we want our children not to be short-changed and, sequentially, avoid perpetuating a culture of mediocrity. So the critical message is, "Don't dummy-down the children." Be wise, strong, courageous, self-sacrificing if necessary, and build children up, inspire them, edify them; give them high standards, values, and expectations so they can be everything they can be, and perhaps everything we wished we could be.

One other point. In my professional teaching career I've seen parents sacrifice their children's aspirations on the alter of their (the parent's) egos. To me this is not only shameful but parentally criminal. If a parent wants to fail, fine. If he or she wants to lead a low life, fine; to be ignoble and violate basic tenets of decency and good character, fine. But for a parent or parents to drag their children down with them is irrefutably unconscionable. As I've said before, if we choose to bring children into this world then we have a sacred obligation to help them have as substantive, whole, happy, and healthy a life as possible, even if that means sacrificing our own lives, ambitions, pleasures, and egos in the process.

Teaching Tips

1. Do not accept any concept, thought, or action that dummies down children. Life is challenging enough for them without having their parents, teachers, friends, or others lowering their expectations, standards, and values. As parents, we need to uplift and support our children.

2. Promote every concept, thought, and action that builds children up, inspires them, strengthens them, and inculcates in them the venerable qualities of exceptionalism, virtue, nobility, confidence, and self-esteem.

3. As our children grow, we need to teach them not to dummy-down others, but rather to edify and encourage them in the process of positive values and a substantive life style.

4. If our children become upset because someone is trying to dummy them down, we need to remind our children to be strong, to focus on their own goodness, and not worry about what others say.

Don't Rush In

Inevitably when our children experience a crisis or have to fight some type of battle, be it emotional, social, psychological, physical, or financial, our immediate response as parents is often to rush in and protect them. My suggestion is, *don't rush in*. If the threat to our children places them in eminent danger, our immediate help is warranted, but otherwise we would be wise to sit back and assess the situation before jumping in to save the day.

The purpose of loving our children is to strengthen them, not weaken them. If we rush in to protect our children every time they encounter a problem in their lives, we will cripple them, not strengthen them. We will also deny them the opportunity to stand on their own two feet and be counted as one who is strong, capable, confident, and willing to confront any challenge, anytime, anywhere, under any circumstances and to do so with courage and an indomitable will to overcome any adversity.

As any martial arts instructor knows, the only way to learn how to fight is to fight. One doesn't learn to fight by avoiding conflict, shying away from adversity, or turning tail and running away. Of course, proper instruction and supervision in how to fight is the best way to learn to defend oneself, but the truth is quite clear – we cannot learn to be competent, confident, and capable through avoidance. There is no other way – we must engage the battle to win the battle.

Martial arts is life. There is nothing we teach in martial arts training that does not have some corresponding aspect in everyday life. For example, when we learn to fight, we are actually learning how to manage adversity, not just a physical adversary.

Life problems are nothing more than adversaries. Therefore, by not rushing in to defend or save our children when they have this or that problem (adversary) we are allowing them the critically positive experience of fighting their own battles, learning how to do things for themselves, to stand up and manage the problem at hand effectively. If we deny them this golden opportunity to learn by themselves while they are under the aegis of our parental protection, they may well grow up as weak, timid, fearful, defensive, incapable adults. Is this what we want as parents for our children?

Again, this is where martial arts training is so powerful. It teaches people to stand up and be strong, and it does this by making them responsible for their own success. No one is holding their hand when they learn to fight, i.e., to challenge adversity. They do it by themselves. After years of study, practice, and applied skills, they become very knowledgeable and capable. The beauty of such training is that individuals intrinsically transfer these skills to everyday life, expertise which becomes an integral part of their very being. The confidence of children to manage life's challenges cannot be learned when a parent or teacher rushes in and fights their fights for them. Children learn how to fight by fighting their own battles. This is truth.

When our children are beset with problems and challenges, we should talk with them about their issues, offer some managerial ideas, and then let the children go out and engage, even embrace, whatever adversities face them. If they don't succeed at first, we should offer more ideas, and then let them go out and confront the problem again. When they succeed, as they will if they keep trying and challenging their fears, the confidence they acquire will be a beautiful thing to behold, and we will have done our job as parents.

To see a child learn to stand up and be counted, to learn to exercise his or her own abilities, and to engage life's challenges face to face with aplomb is absolutely wonderful. Such confidence and beauty will never be theirs if we parents rush in and solve every problem for them in their lives. If we continually play the savior in their childhood, we may well regret it in their adulthood. Do we really want our children coming back to us to help them stand on their own two feet when they're adults? I think not. Therefore, we should monitor our impulses to rush in every time our kids face a challenge.

Teaching Tips

1. Discipline yourself to not rush in every time your child has a problem. Give them a chance to figure it out on their own. When they fall down when learning to walk, for example, don't rush to pick them up, and don't let your face express concern. If you do, they will automatically reflect that concern and fear. Rather, just ignore them or simply encourage them to get back up and keep going. Don't overreact. React with positive assertion and confidence, emboldening them with a courageous spirit. Doing this when children are learning to walk teaches them they can solve their own life's problems. However, if we run to them, pick them up, and excessively fuss as to whether they are hurt or not, we will reinforce their inability to do things for themselves. In effect, we will be crippling them. Children catch on very quickly. If you react with positive power, they will do likewise.

Children copy their parents. Therefore, let them copy strength, confidence, and personal power.

2. As children grow they will possibly have social issues. Teach them through continual positive reinforcement as they mature that they are whole, strong, capable, courageous, and competent individuals, and they do not need anyone else's approval to define or validate them. When children are different, or they become achievers, they will become targets for the ridicule of others. If we teach them how complete they are in their own right, they won't be affected by the derisive or denigrating remarks of others. Teach them that just as there is day and night, there are positive people and negative people and to consider the source, ignore it, and move on. Certainly encourage them to make their own decisions and to not allow someone else's criticisms or vituperations to affect them negatively.

First Comes Ticker

As parents, our goal is to do all we can to raise our children to live a meaningful and substantive life, but where do we begin? My own children will tell you that I was emphatic with them that everything begins with *ticker*.

What is *ticker*? Ticker is the beating and expression of the heart, of love and compassion. As a father, I would tell my children this:

> *Whatever you become in life, if you do not have a loving heart, you are nothing.*

Seems pretty severe, doesn't it? Yet, I believe it to be the most important quality of being a successful and substantive human being. Anyone can be accomplished at a particular skill, but not everyone will have the humility and spirituality to be compassionate, loving, and caring – first, not second. I'm pleased to say that my children have grown to be exceptional people, as well as loving, caring, compassionate parents.

How many adults have become successful in a line of work but failed miserably in being a loving individual? It's far easier to succeed at a thing or occupation than it is to make *ticker* your primary motivation as a parent or individual.

What is the first thing all high level mystics, saints, and spiritual scriptures teach? It is love. Why? Because love exudes a mindset that has the highest and best good of others, especially children, at its core. Yet, worldly success is often gained at the expense of others, not through the love of others. How many fortunes in this world have been made, are being made, and will be made through untoward means involving dishonesty, deceit, treachery, greed, ego, miserliness, stinginess, or viciousness?

Sir John Dalberg-Acton, known as Lord Acton, was one of the greatest and most learned personalities of the 19th Century. In a letter to Bishop Mandell Creighton in 1887, Lord Acton penned a phrase that has become universally recognized:

> *Power tends to corrupt, and absolute power corrupts absolutely. Great men are almost always bad men.*

Notice the correlation Acton makes between "great" men and "bad" men. Much of the time they are synonymous. This begs the question, "Why does the world often assign the title "great men" to bad or nefarious men?"

Think of those "great" men who have, throughout history, built empires by slaughtering, raping, plundering, and destroying other human beings for their own aggrandizement and "greatness." Is this really greatness?

Who are those among us who are truly great, who have the highest and best good of others in their hearts? What parents place their children's success and well-being before their (the parent's) own success? How many children today would say their parents put them first, who sacrificed their lives for them? How many children grow up to be troubled adults because their parents were not concerned with them, the children? I dare say the archives of humanity are littered with parents who placed themselves, their well-being, and their "greatness" before their children. The allure of worldly fame, celebrity, power, success, and notoriety are powerful opiates. Yet, they are garbage in relation to the radiance of loving parents who place their children's success and well-being above their own.

This brings us back to *ticker* – the beating of the heart and its love. There is nothing greater in this world than love. Money can't buy it. Love stands alone as the highest expression of a human being. Hence, the reason for the statement:

> *Whatever you become in life, if you do not have a loving heart, you are nothing.*

Teaching Tips

1. Begin from the get-go in raising your children by telling them that their self-worth as a human being begins with *ticker*, i.e., with love. You will never regret doing so. Just about everything in this world can be purchased except love. It is priceless.

2. Read stories to children of loving souls. Talk to them about people who are loving, kind, and compassionate. Establish a foundation of love early on.

3. Of course, be the *living example* of love, compassion, and sacrifice for your children (see *Be A Living Example*).

4. Teach your children to think of others, to be helpful, kind, considerate, thoughtful, tender.

5. When concepts of success arise in the maturation phrase of your children's lives, make sure they understand that love is the first ingredient of being successful – not fame, name, fortune, or celebrity. Place love first, foremost, and forever. It is love that is a manifestation of the divine spark within each of us. Money, name, and fame are merely inconsequential and ephemeral trappings of an inconsequential and ephemeral world. Within the grand scope of life, the most consequential quality is *ticker*.

Give 'Em A Spine

For children to become whole, they need to be strong, to have the ability to stand up and speak up for what they believe in whether other people think they are wrong or not. They also need to have the grit and courage to act on their principles, not just give them lip service. Therefore, it is important to *Give 'Em A Spine*.

Eleanor Roosevelt, the wife of American President Franklin D. Roosevelt, was the longest-serving First Lady of the United States (1933 to 1945). Her following statement is quite appropriate to having a spine.

> *Do what you feel in your heart to be right – for you'll be criticized anyway. You'll be damned if you do, and damned if you don't.*

In order for our children to have a spine, a backbone, the resolve to stand up and be counted, even if one's views are unpopular or go against the grain of popular opinion, Eleanor Roosevelt's statement offers a strong tool for having strength and courage. No matter what someone says, he or she will be criticized. Therefore, stand up and speak up. Honor that spine.

A world leader with great substance was Winston Churchill who is arguably to Great Britain what Abraham Lincoln is to the United States. He was a powerful and highly effective leader, especially during England's darkest hours of World War II. Churchill served twice as Prime Minister of Great Britain: 1940-1945 and 1951-1955.

Two of Churchill's statements in his treasure trove of memorable quotes are:

> *You have enemies? Good. That means you've stood up for something, sometime in your life.*

and . . .

> *Courage is what it takes to stand up and speak; courage is also what it takes to sit down and listen.*

Another of Great Britain's distinguished leaders and Prime Ministers was Margaret Thatcher, known as the "Iron Lady" for her noteworthy stalwartness. She served her country in its highest post from 1979 to 1990. The first of her two quotes below is important for children, especially teenagers, who often are more concerned with popularity than substance.

> *If you just set out to be liked, you would be prepared to compromise on anything at any time, and you would achieve nothing.*

Another excellent "Iron Lady" quotation speaks to the longevity of having a spine.

> *You may have to fight a battle more than once to win it.*

Helping our children to develop a spine means that while they are maturing they should not be denied any opportunity to stand up for themselves, even if doing so causes them stress and discomfort. Strength, like muscle, is made stronger under weight-bearing activity. This is why athletics involve an assortment of strength and conditioning exercises. If we want to have strong bodies, we have to condition them with the stress of weight and physical conditioning. If we want to have a strong character and set of ethics, we have to embrace those situations in life with the weight of challenges which, although uncomfortable, make us stronger. So it is with our children. We must not shield them from those events that strengthen their spine.

One of the world's most famous individuals of the 19th/20th Centuries was Helen Keller. If anyone can speak to the quality of having a spine and its attending courage and grit, it is she. Her following thoughts are apropos.

> *We could never learn to be brave and patient if there were only joy in the world.*

and . . .

> *Character cannot be developed in ease and quiet. Only through experience of trial and suffering can the soul be strengthened, ambition inspired, and success achieved.*

Having a spine is not a transitory aspect of one's character. Having a spine is a life-long function and necessity if one is to lead a substantive life. It is much easier to develop as a child than as an adult, just as it's easier for a child to learn multiple languages than an adult. Having a strong spine will keep our children free by allowing them to stand up to the mental and emotional assaults of others and life in general.

Teaching Tips

1. A child should never be denied the opportunity to develop a spine, regardless of how uncomfortable it is for the child. If it's not "then," then when? Every instance in which a child could have been taught to stand up for himself and didn't is an opportunity lost.

2. When parents are aware of such a "spine-strengthening" occasion confronting their child, it would be wise first of all for them not to overreact and rush to the child's defense (see the segment *Don't Rush In*).

3. Role playing is an excellent teaching tool. Create a game in which you (the parent) are going to play a bully or a naughty person and your child is going to stand up to you, the bully. Your child's reaction does not have to be mean or vicious. It just has to be positive, firm, and assertive. By playing such games, the child will be conditioned as to how to respond should he ever be put upon by someone else in an untoward manner.

4. When there are conversations in the family, encourage children to offer their point of view. Do not use the philosophy, "Children are to be seen and not heard," which was a standard parenting philosophy in times past. Rather, let the children have a voice. If, as a parent, we do not give our children the opportunity of having a voice or developing their spine, how will they ever learn to stand up for themselves and be strong?

5. We must be cautious of being too soft on our children. We don't want them to hurt, but life is full of hurts. Our best way to protect them against the hurts is to *Give 'Em A Spine* and teach them how to stand on their own two feet, have confidence, be balanced, and be counted.

Grown Ups, Own Up

If there is any one thing that separates "grown ups" from children it is that *Grown Ups, Own Up*. Adults take responsibility for their own actions and do not blame others for their choices or lot in life. As the famous Indian Saint, Guru Nanak (the first of the ten Sikh Gurus), emphatically stated:

> *I blame not another, I blame my own karmas. Whatever I sowed, so did I reap. Why then put the blame on others?*

This is exactly what Grown Ups do – they take responsibility for their lives because they understand the great law of Cause and Effect, Sowing and Reaping, Karma.

Corroborating Guru Nanak's statement, Saint Dadu Dayal remarked:

> *What thou hast not done will never befall thee; only what thou hast done will befall thee.*

Translated into modern speech, Dadu's statement would read:

> *What you have not done will never happen to you; only what you have done will happen to you.*

So it goes with all highly evolved souls. They understand that what happens to them is by their own hand, by their own doing. They never blame others because to blame others would be to deny the science and reality of life. Saints know, and all mature individuals know, that to be an adult means to take responsibility for oneself and one's actions, i.e., *Grown Ups, Own Up.*

It may seem obvious that adult individuals own up to their own lives and actions, but is this true? How many Grown Ups actually own up to their lives, choices, circumstances, responsibilities, obligations, financial conditions, and relationship interactions? Furthermore, and more importantly, how many Grown Ups are truly accountable and responsible for their mistakes, faults, failings, and shortcomings?

We live in an age where *owning up* seems to be a dying virtue, like so many other virtues. It's so easy to pass the buck and blame someone else. We see such adolescent behavior in all walks of life and even at the pinnacle of those in the hallowed halls of leadership. And that is exactly what passing the buck is – adolescent. It is not adult behavior. It is childish behavior. Just because a person lives in a biologically adult body does not make him or her an adult. Why? Because *Grown Ups, Own Up*, and being "grown up" means owning up and being accountable for one's actions.

Teaching Tips

1. When kids begin to approach their teen years, it's time to begin stressing and reinforcing the *Grown Ups, Own Up* maxim. Too many kids today, in spite of growing into biologically mature bodies, are not growing into a mature adult mindset. It takes maturity to be an adult, not simply age.

2. Every time a child is confronted with a choice, remind him or her of the consequences of that choice, and do your best to guide him or her to the right choice. Don't overdo it but do keep the concept of *Grown Ups, Own Up* constantly before them until they become its manifestation. This harmonizes with *Your Life, Your Responsibility*, and so many of the other concepts featured in this work, especially those related to personal character.

High Bar, High Life
Low Bar, Low Life

To have a high life, we have to have a high bar. High lives are noble lives, magnanimous lives, substantive lives, virtuous lives, lives which have meaning and give life to life itself.

High lives transcend material, monetary, celebratory, status-driven success. How many rich, famous, and socially powerful individuals throughout history have led lives of a superficial, destructive, degenerative, negative nature?

High lives are built on character, service, humanity, spirituality, and virtue. These are qualities devoid of material or worldly attachment. Anyone can have a high life because all things noble reflect a consciousness that is edified and elevated.

The famous Chinese philosopher Confucius, who lived between 551-479 BCE (Before the Common Era), in his work *The Confucian Analects* states:

> *The superior man thinks always of virtue; the common man thinks of comfort.*

> *Without recognizing the ordinances of Heaven, it is impossible to be a superior man.*

Dr. Albert Einstein noted:

> *The highest destiny of the individual is to serve rather than to rule. Try not to become a man of success but rather to become a man of value.*

> *Not everything that can be counted counts, and not everything that counts can be counted.*

Benjamin Franklin commented:

> *There was never yet a truly great man that was not at the same time truly virtuous.*

> *Only a virtuous people are capable of freedom.*

Unfortunately, we live in an age where the bar of life continues to drop lower and lower, miserably lower, shamefully lower, destructively lower. Virtue, for example, is denigrated, ridiculed, criticized. If a young person were to refuse to engage in sexual relations before marriage, he or she would be mocked mercilessly, rather than being applauded and supported for demonstrating such virtuous conduct, and virtuous conduct it is, irrefutably.

Perhaps this is why Edward Dahlberg, a 20th Century American novelist, critic, and essayist observed:

> *Nothing in our times has become so unattractive as virtue.*

In contrast, Saint Kabir (15th/16th Centuries) affirms:

> *The wicked look on virtue with contempt for sinning is to them so great a pleasure.*

The ancient Greek teacher and philosopher Socrates stated:

> *It is the greatest good for an individual to discuss virtue every day . . . for the unexamined life is not worth living.*

If an individual is upright, honest, direct, kind, helpful, compassionate, and does his best to continually elevate his consciousness, ethics, conduct, and do good deeds, he is often scorned and treated as a pariah, a goody-two-shoes. Hence, the famous quote from 20th Century author, editor, playwright, and diplomat, Clare Booth Luce:

> *No good deed goes unpunished.*

In concert with Luce's comment, Mark Twain poignantly writes:

> *Be good and you will be lonely.*

Modern day life is overflowing with examples of the bar being lowered every day. It is sad and tragic, but it does not mean individuals have to succumb to such a depreciating universal mindset or that parents have to accept such a lowering of standards. Quite the contrary.

High bars create high lives. Low bars create low lives. It's impossible to get a high life from a low bar, and the lower the bar continues to sink, the harder it is to climb.

There is a common erroneous thought in this culture that one should not strive for perfection. The supposition is that we're all imperfect so why try to be perfect? This is, certainly, one reason why mankind continues to descend into ever-increasing depths of mediocrity and darkness. Argue for your limitations and they're yours. State your possibilities and they are yours as well. As Buddha clearly and sagaciously stated: *What we think, we become.*

One of the most famous, and glorious, books of the 1970s is *Jonathan Livingston Seagull* by Richard Bach. It is a classic, and one which every person striving to excel should read and have in his or her library. Following are a few of the inspiring quotations from that work.

> *Heaven is being perfect.*

> *The gull sees farthest who flies highest.*

> *Do you have any idea how many lives we must have gone through before we even got the first idea that there is more to life than eating or fighting, or power in the Flock? A thousand lives, Jon, ten thousand! And then another hundred lives until we began to learn that there is such a thing as perfection, and another hundred again to get the idea that our purpose for living is to find that perfection and show it forth.*

The Bible strongly professes the directive of being perfect. Genesis 17:1 reads:

> *And when Abram was ninety years old and nine, the Lord appeared to Abram, and said unto him, I am the Almighty God; walk before me, and be thou perfect.*

St. Matthew 5:48 confirms the same principle:

> *Be ye therefore perfect, even as your Father which is in heaven is perfect.*

Saint Jagat Singh echoes the same universal truth:

> *Be as perfect as your creator.*

The theme of *perfection* and *being perfect* is requisite to a high bar and a high life. It is universal, spanning all civilizations, cultures, people, ages, and eras. Perfection can never be separated from the human spirit because it is the human spirit. It is that intrinsically divine spark embedded within every cell of our very being – an eternal, undying, indomitable divine ray of living energy that relentlessly inspires us to move, not just forward but upward.

Unfortunately, in our world there are and will always be those individuals who seek to ridicule, mock, castigate, denigrate, defame, or in some way attack perfection and virtue. Because of this sad reality we should fortify our children against such negativity by teaching them that virtue, noble actions, and a substantive character are the attributes of truly great souls.

Joseph Addison, a 17th/18th Century British essayist, poet, playwright, and politician speaks directly to this issue when he says:

> *Ridicule is generally made use of to laugh men out of virtue and good sense by attacking everything praiseworthy in human life.*

Addison's wisdom should act as a shield for perfection-seeking, virtuous-minded individuals against the onslaught of misguided souls and their nefarious machinations. Virtue and perfection must never be subjugated to the dark energy of ridicule or the people who spew it.

Nobility is one of the most worthy poems addressing a high life. It was written by 19th Century American poetess, Alice Carey.

Nobility

Alice Carey

True worth is in being, not seeming,
In doing, each day that goes by,
Some little good—not in dreaming
Of great things to do by and by.
For whatever men say in their blindness,
And spite of the fancies of youth,
There's nothing so kingly as kindness,
And nothing so royal as truth.

We get back our mete as we measure;
We cannot do wrong and feel right,
Nor can we give pain and gain pleasure,
For justice avenges each slight.
The air for the wing of the sparrow,
The bush for the robin and wren,
But always the path that is narrow
And straight, for the children of men.

'Tis not in the pages of story
The heart of its ills to beguile,
Though he who makes courtship to glory
Gives all that he hath for her smile.
For when from her heights he has won her,
Alas! it is only to prove
That nothing's so sacred as honor,
And nothing so loyal as love!

We cannot make bargains for blisses,
Nor catch them like fishes in nets;
And sometimes the thing our life misses
Helps more than the thing which it gets.
For good lieth not in pursuing,
Nor gaining of great nor of small,
But just in the doing, and doing
As we would be done by, is all.

Through envy, through malice, through hating,
Against the world, early and late,
No jot of our courage abating
Our part is to work and to wait,
And slight is the sting of his trouble
Whose winnings are less than his worth,
For he who is honest is noble
Whatever his fortunes or birth.

Teaching Tips

1. Set a high bar for your children, high expectations. Do not succumb to the limiting mindset of the masses which continually seeks mediocrity.

2. Encourage children to memorize quotations from noble and great individuals to act as a shield against those who seek to cast a negative net over the ideals of perfection, virtue, and nobility.

3. Create a foundation of excellence in your children by pointing out the excellence in others.

4. Praise excellence in your own children, even in the little things. Never criticize, ridicule, or demean them. Bolster, support, and strengthen them through positive and uplifting

words and actions. Share stories and quotations with them from great people throughout history.

5. While encouraging your children to set, and reach, high bars, teach them never to disparage others or look down upon them in any way. Such behavior would obviously betray conduct befitting a high, noble, exalted life and character.

How To Spoil A Child

Spoiling children is easy, a lot easier than raising them responsibly. The rub is that although it may be easier for parents in the short-term, the long-term effects can be disastrous and of no help to the child growing into adulthood.

When we spoil children we are not helping them to be independent, strong, whole, substantive individuals. In fact, we are crippling them, actually creating a weak foundation that will not support the rigorous demands of an adult life, its challenges and responsibilities. Consider how some buildings with a weak structural foundation react in an earthquake. They collapse.

If we want the best for our children, we must guard against spoiling them because spoiling is exactly that – spoiling, i.e., creating rotten fruit. And what do most people do with spoiled, rotten fruit? They throw it out, discard it into the garbage. Why? Simply because spoiled fruit has no intrinsic value and can be dangerously unhealthy.

There are many ways to spoil children. Following is a brief list of things to do *if* you want to spoil your child or children. I'm sure you can also make your own list.

1. Do everything for them
2. Never make them take responsibility for their actions
3. Never establish boundaries, borders, rules, regulations
4. Never take charge as a parent
5. Never demand your children show respect to others
6. Placate them rather than discipline them

7. Tell them they're always great regardless of their performance
8. Be inconsistent in your parental directives
9. Don't make them work for anything
10. Bail them out of trouble when you ought not to
11. Make life too easy for them
12. Overprotect them
13. Not force them to learn some basic manners
14. Give them everything they want
15. Not force them to clean up their rooms or their messes
16. Not make them stand on their own two feet
17. Tell them their self-generated problems are not their fault
18. Not make them own up when they mess up
19. Refuse to discipline them when they deserve it
20. Allow them to misbehave in public

Teaching Tips

1. Study the above list.
2. Set an example for your children.
3. Be consistent in disciplining them.
4. Be conscious of your own parenting weaknesses and make adjustments where necessary.

It's Not All About Them

One of the problematic conditions affecting many young people today is that they erroneously believe the world revolves around them. This has always been a teenage issue, but it's expanding beyond the teen years into adulthood. Such self-centeredness is not only myopic but deleterious to a person's future because, obviously, the world does not revolve around any one individual, notwithstanding any delusions to the contrary.

There was a time in world history when mainline human thought was that the earth was the center of the universe. This geocentric philosophy was disproven by Nicolaus Copernicus in the 16th Century through the concept of heliocentricity in which the sun was the center of the then known universe.

Today it seems as though a social geocentricity in the form of egocentricity is intensifying throughout the globe. The manifested energy in the forms of *I*, *me*, *my,* and *mine* dominate entities – individual, political, cultural, national. Thus, from a human standpoint, and in a manner of speaking, the world is still functioning in a pre-Copernican geocentric mindset.

Such a state of affairs is not surprising, for as 15th/16th Century Saint Ravidas declared:

> *The world is a house of collyrium (an abode of evil), a veritable well of the poison of egotism.*

Yet, as parents we would serve our children best if we taught them that they are not the center of the universe, figuratively speaking of course. There are other people in the world who have differing cultures, languages, beliefs, philosophies, customs, and governmental systems.

In reality, none of us is so special as to believe the world, even our personal world, revolves around us. Think of how massive the universe is as we know it. Science tells us there are more stars in the universe than all the grains of sand on all the beaches of the world!

Have you ever attempted to count the number of grains of sand in a simple thimble? As a teenager, I started to do that once. I went to the beach, collected a thimble full of sand, went home, poured the sand out on the kitchen table, began to count the grains of sand, and I quit within the first minute. There was no way I was going to sit there and count every one of those sand particles!

In my aborted attempt I began to think about each of those grains of sand as a sun, a star. Then I thought about all the beaches in the world and all the potential grains of sand on those beaches. Next, I thought about the potential of each of those grains being a sun and having solar systems with worlds like our own revolving around them.

Moving further into the depths of this thought process, I thought about all the potential living beings residing on each of those worlds revolving around each of those suns. Then I thought about our own Milky Way galaxy and the billions of stars it alone contained, a galaxy which is one of billions of galaxies in our universe, the end to which we haven't even discovered!

I couldn't wrap my mind around the immensity of it all, and I felt small, so small that I couldn't even imagine myself as a speck of dust on a speck of dust. How infinitesimal I was, how insignificant. My self-importance as a teenager immediately shifted to zero importance. In the grand scheme of things I was nothing, and I still maintain this thought to this day.

And so it was, at least for me. But I wonder how many teenagers still think of themselves as important. I wonder why so many adults are still consumed with their own egos. The bottom line is that in the big picture of life each of us is so small, so miniscule, that we're basically nothing.

So why do we often think we're everything? What have we not been taught in life that keeps us so ego-entrenched? What have we taught our children that they should feel so self-consumed, self-important, egocentric? What have we missed? What have our children missed?

The reality of life as I have come to know and experience through my own life experiences and professional numerology work is that there is an intelligent universal power so vast that it transcends the comprehension of the human mind. This power rests at the core of everything, is everything. When this power is everything, how can we be anything? Yet, we continue to parade through life like strutting peacocks, celebratory gods, and statuesque inamorata. In doing so we have furthered the delusion of our own self-importance.

As parents who believe in helping our children rise to their highest and best good, I believe it's important to keep them balanced. Certainly one way to do this is help them understand life from a universal macroscopic point of view rather than from a microscopic one. We are all part of life. We derive our existence from one Power. Therefore, how can any of us be all that superior to another? Beyond being a speck of dust on a speck of dust, we have no more worth than a bubble on the ocean.

Adopting this point of view will help us and our children become more humble for, indeed, humility is the highest form of strength; arrogance the highest form of weakness.

Pause for a moment and consider those individuals throughout history who have been truly great. They are all humble. They don't salivate in their own self-importance but remain steadfastly connected to a higher power, a higher cause, a higher calling. They are not self-absorbed but spiritually and universally absorbed. Great talents may have come through them but not from them, for they recognize the divine and sacred energy within all people, all souls. Is teaching this concept to our children not in their highest and best good? Of course it is.

However we do it, it is important to teach children the dangers of becoming too self-absorbed. So many problems in life are created when egos get out of control. In fact, stop and think how many of life's everyday problems are the direct result of ego. Too many to count, just like the grains of sand on the beaches of the world.

Life is much bigger than any of us. No one is "all that." We are all part of a greater whole. Thinking in such terms will help keep our children's perspective of life in balance and their egos in check – their lives becoming more substantive in the process, while avoiding life's traps and snares.

Teaching Tips

1. We should help our children understand their own intrinsic self-worth but guard against making them think the world revolves around them because it doesn't.

2. Be careful of praising children when they don't deserve it, but do praise them when their behavior warrants it.

3. Too much praise can lead to self-delusion and narcissism. Big heads are like balloons expanded beyond their acceptable elasticity, popping at the slightest pin prick.

4. Let us not forget the age-old maxim, *The bigger they are, the harder they fall.* If we don't want our children to have a Humpty-Dumpty life, it would be wise for us to teach them to take the high road but the low ground. In other words, live a noble life but a humble one.

Living With Grace

Life is difficult, no question. As Buddha says:

Existence is suffering.

Saint Ravidas remarks:

This world is a field of suffering.

Saint Sawan Singh observes:

This world is the plane of struggle.

We all suffer in this life, but how we manage our suffering defines our level of consciousness and spiritual maturity. When we are beset with extreme challenges, do we bewail our woes and lament our misfortunes openly, or do we remain balanced, centered, calm, and resolute while accepting the slings and arrows of life, continuing to press on with a relentlessly positive, grateful, gracious, and imperturbable spirit?

One of the measures of a mature, whole, and balanced individual is how well he or she deals with adversity. Certainly, more advanced souls live their lives with grace – a most beautiful expression of an elevated consciousness.

Grace is divinity in manifestation. It is love, kindness, compassion, centeredness, humility, poise, aplomb, acceptance, resolve, and patience merged into a symphony of exquisite magnificence.

Grace is that quality which, in spite of hardships, setbacks, failures, disappointments, tragedies, and unspeakable tears, never complains, bemoans, or bewails its misfortunes but endures them and presses on in an unwavering attitude of divine acceptance without drawing attention to itself.

To have grace is to exude a sense of manners and decorum, to be poised and refined, polished and positive, gentle and generous, to have beauty and breeding, breeding which is based on noble actions, not social status or riches.

As our children grow, they will experience problems. An assortment of heartaches, heartbreaks, storms, tribulations, and challenges are built into the fabric of everyone's destiny. Some people have greater degrees of challenge and turmoil in their lives than others but no one is exempt. If our children are to live life nobly we need to instill in them the quality of grace.

The revered Greek teacher and philosopher Aristotle (384 B.C. – 322 B.C.) wrote:

> *The ideal man bears the accidents of life with dignity and grace, making the best of circumstances.*

The famous Roman philosopher, statesman, and playwright Seneca, whose full name is Lucius Annaeus Seneca (4 B.C. – A.D. 65), stated:

We should give as we would receive, cheerfully, quickly, and without hesitation; for there is no grace in a benefit that sticks to the fingers.

Jonathan Edwards, one of the most noteworthy theologians in American history (18th Century), wrote:

Grace is but glory begun, and glory is but grace perfected.

Grace is a virtue. It is good to live with grace. It makes us noble, whole, and grand. If we want our children to shine and be exemplary human beings, then we need to teach them to live their lives with grace and to be gracious.

There will be no dearth of opportunities in our children's lives to teach them grace, especially in athletics and competitive endeavors. Everyone loses at some time in life, and it is defeat which offers one of the most powerful teaching moments a parent or child can have. Anyone can have grace and be gracious in victory, but it is in defeat that one's true character shines.

Teaching Tips

1. If we parents can reflect grace in our lives, then our beloved children will have a working model by which to pattern their lives. Life begets life; grace begets grace. We do not get life from death nor grace from disgrace.

2. When children experience setbacks, failures, etc., point out to them how beautifully whole, strong, and noble it makes them when they deal with such adversity with grace. Tell them directly that the greatest of all people are those who exhibit grace, especially in difficult times.

3. When your children lose a competitive event, encourage them to remain positive, giving sincere congratulatory praise to the victor. This will actually make them a winner. Thus, even in defeat the loser triumphs! What should not be done in defeat is to grumble, whine, complain, and diminish the victor. Such behavior only further diminishes the vanquished, while making him look small and petty, neither grand nor great. To be great is to applaud the victor, graciously, or, in triumph, to be gracious.

Make It A Game

Correcting children's behavior is a necessary and prominent aspect of parenting. As all vines need trimming so they don't grow into an unruly wild mess, so do children. Trimming, shaping, and sculpting children's conduct is critical to their well-being and future lives. How the shaping is done is key to success.

One excellent strategy I've learned through my professional teaching and parenting development is to *make it a game*. Kids love games, so rather than using harsh or uncomfortable measures to correct behavior, especially when children are young, simply create a game for them in which they can learn the correct and desired behavior, albeit indirectly and without you divulging your methods to them.

Still As Stone

For example, we parents know that children can have a challenging time being still from time to time, right? (I can hear you laughing.) So how can we parents first get them to settle down and then teach them to be still?

One tactic I've used successfully without fail is to play the *still as stone* game. Here's how it works. You begin by joyfully exclaiming to your child or children, "Let's play a game!" Because kids love games, they more often than not respond with excitement. Then you say, "Let's play *still as stone*." You direct them to sit down, placing their hands in their laps. Then you say slowly and dramatically, maybe even whispering, "Now let's see if you can not move a muscle and be as "still as stone" for just ten seconds. If you can do this, you win! Okay?" Make being still a big deal to underscore its importance.

As a note, it's good to get children's confirmation before starting the game because it makes them part of the process. It's inclusive. Then you direct them to close their eyes and be as "still as stone" for ten seconds. You say, "Ready, go!" You can even count the seconds out loud, and probably should in the beginning because it will give the children an audible marker to judge their impending success. If they do not move in that ten second period, i.e., if they remain "still as stone," then you say excitedly, "Wow! You won! Congratulations!" If they move at all, then you tell them they didn't win, and then do it again until they succeed. After all, ten seconds is not very long, but the idea of success is powerful because almost all children love to succeed. It's a natural process. After they succeed with a ten second time period, keep extending the time until they can do it for two, three, or five minutes. Build success in small steps.

If a child balks at playing such a game, especially if it's a boy (because that's just how boys are), you ask, "Are you strong enough to be still?" This immediately appeals to and challenges his innate sense of power, strength, courage, and developing manhood. What male does not want to be powerful, strong, and courageous?

This *still as stone* game works. Its success has been duplicated innumerable times in my decades of teaching and parenting. It has great merit because it not only is fun, it teaches children to be still and to develop discipline and self-control in a way that is totally acceptable and positive – discipline and self-control every human being needs in order to have a safe, meaningful, and substantive life.

Still as stone also creates a sense of personal success in children. Every time they succeed and you make it a big deal, especially in the beginning, their confidence grows because their competence grows, and *competence creates confidence.*

Another advantage of *still as stone* is that it indirectly establishes the parent or teacher as the leader and authority figure. This further cements parental control but in an indirect and totally unobtrusive way. Everybody wins. The children gain a feeling of success while they learn to discipline and control themselves. Parents win because they not only help their kids to mature through little success steps, but they (the parents) get some quiet time, oftentimes a valuable commodity for them. (I sense heads nodding.)

Beat the Teacher or Parent

Another powerfully successful game technique is to have children compete with their parent or teacher. Kids love any game in which they have the opportunity to whip their teachers and parents. Their competitive instincts are noticeably energized when they have a chance to "beat the teacher" or "beat the parent."

The key to *beat the teacher* or *beat the parent* is to allow the child to ultimately win the game (whatever the game is) in order to build the child's competence and his or her succeeding confidence. We should not make the game too easy, however. That would defeat the purpose. The purpose is to develop the child's confidence by having him or her engage in a challenging process in which they have to work to win. If victory is given too easily or too soon, children will not develop the grit, determination, focus, and wherewithal that is needed to succeed in life's greater challenges, which they most certainly will encounter at some point in life, as we all do. Nobody's life is totally easy. Challenge and struggle are part of being human. Therefore, by teaching children to be strong and determined will be to their great benefit. Beating the teacher or parent is a fun, supportive game by which to achieve this goal.

The sky's the limit as far as what games to play. It's all a matter of imagination. The goal is for children to face adversity, challenge it, struggle against it, and ultimately triumph in the end. It's a process of learning to be strong, competent, and confident.

Stop And Go

Another game which also teaches discipline and self-control is called *stop and go*, or as it is also known, *red light, green light*. One of its great benefits is that it also teaches children to *listen* closely to directions, i.e., to *concentrate* on what is being said and behave accordingly.

Here's how it's played. Have children line up in a horizontal straight line. This will be the start line. Create an end line several feet or yards away. When you say, "Go," the children walk forward. When you say, "Stop," they stop. The goal is to get to the finish line. If they don't stop on time, they have to go back to the start line. This teaches them that life has consequences, but it's so innocuous that the lesson – to listen, have discipline, self-control, and that actions have consequences – will go totally unnoticed. Kids don't know they're learning valuable life skills. To them, they're just playing a game and having fun!

To give *stop and go* more variety, introduce varying ways for the children to move from the start line to the finish line. For example, rather than have them walk, have them hop on two legs, maybe hop on one leg. They can also jump, crawl, or run (distance permitting). They can also do each drill backward to make it even more challenging.

Simon Says

We've all played *Simon Says*. It's a universal game, and it's a valuable teaching technique for kids as well as adults because in order to win the game and beat "Simon" (the authority figure) the participants have to not only listen very carefully but combine their listening acumen with their visual acuity. It also teaches competitive excellence because if a participant does not do what Simon says, he has to sit down until the game is over and a winner is determined.

Simon Says is the number one teaching tool in my game chest that I've used throughout my professional martial arts career and parenting life. Even adults love it and ask to play it because it sharpens their concentration, hearing and seeing abilities, and . . . it's fun!

There are many ways to make *Simon Says* challenging. Of course for very young kids the difficulty level is quite low. As success is achieved, more complexity can be added in a variety of ways, and should be added because the greater the complexity, the greater the skills needed to succeed, thus leading to greater competence and personal confidence.

As we know, in *Simon Says* the participants can only do what Simon says, not what Simon does. For example, if Simon says, "Raise your right arm," while he raises his left arm in order to trick the participants, any participant who lifts his left arm, not his right arm, loses and has to sit down until the game is concluded with everyone else. This tactic of Simon saying one thing and doing another is one level used to add complexity, challenge, and excitement to the game.

Another layer of complexity is to change the tempo and timing of what is being said. Starting slowly with commands and then speeding up to develop comprehension and reactionary skills creates more challenge.

Yet another wrinkle when playing *Simon Says* is for Simon to use various voices while giving commands, especially if he or she is theatrically inclined. This adds a lot of fun to the game and further forces the participants to listen even more closely than before because varying voices naturally have differing sounds, tones, stress points, inflections, rhythms, and timings.

One of my favorite Simon commands is to tell the participants to stand completely still, keep their eyes open, and not to smile or laugh. This immediately creates a most challenging circumstance because people generally smile and laugh as a natural part of life. Then, with everyone trying to keep from smiling or laughing, I'll do something totally silly in order to break their concentration, such as using different voices, snorting, running up and down the line like a clown, getting face-to-face with people (never touching them because that's not fair in a verbal game), looking directly into their eyes while making funny faces and saying funny things – all designed to get them to break their concentration and either smile or laugh. It's great fun for everyone, and what a powerful teaching technique it is! And what's the payoff for them? The payoff for the participants is learning to listen, think, concentrate, act accordingly, maintain discipline and self-control – all great and useful life skills.

Opposing Advantage

A great advantage of game playing beyond the games themselves and the life skills they teach, is that they establish a clear dichotomy between learning through fun and learning through more strict disciplinary measures, thus increasing the effectiveness of both opposing styles, which in turn makes parenting more effective. In a way it's sort of like "good cop, bad cop."

Life is dual by nature. Teaching and learning can be effective using some techniques that are fun and other techniques that, when needed, are strict, even stern. Parenting efficiency draws upon both strategies.

Children get it. They appreciate it when parents have fun with them and bear no grudge when mom and dad have to be more strict in their approach. Kids appreciate the fun, but in most cases they all know that when they've misbehaved they're going to face some discipline – from simple time-outs to denial of privileges to restriction of some sort.

If a parent has used fun games, for example, as an integral part of the child-raising process, then the children are more likely to be accepting of disciplinary measures when their parents employ them because they (the children) have experienced both *fun love* and *tough love*. This creates balance in their lives. But if raising children is always strict, cold, sterile, stern, detached, and indifferent, then the possibility of children growing up less than happy, whole, and balanced is increased. If there is only *fun love* and no *tough love*, then children are at risk of growing up disrespectful, defiant, entitled, angry, and uncontrolled. Life is not all fun and games, so experiencing only a *fun love* strategy creates an illusion of real life, and when that illusion is shattered, the outcome may well be quite challenging, if not negative and destructive.

Winning Versus Feelings

I'm a little touchy about this subject, so my caveat is to strap in and buckle up if you want to continue reading. I'm not going to pull any punches, so be forewarned.

Speaking of winning as an aspect of game-playing – the concept of everyone being equal and getting a prize and having no winners in a game because of someone's feelings being hurt is totally destructive to developing strong, competent, confident, whole, balanced, rational, realistic, and mature individuals.

Denying success, excellence, and perfection in life to any child at the expense of another child's feelings is utterly wrong and misguided. Such action is not only unnatural, it is unfair, unjust, and serves to undermine the concept of excellence and all that it entails – hard work, effort, focus, discipline, determination, dedication, concentration, courage, strength, adaptability, resourcefulness, resolve, creativity, originality, individuality, imagination, independence, and leadership. Additionally, it denies the child who is not as successful the opportunity to learn, grow, overcome adversity, develop life-enhancing skills, courage, character, independence, and a whole gamut of positive character traits that would better his or her life.

Attempting to make everyone equal is blasphemous to the human spirit and the natural structure of life. The reality of life is that not everyone is going to succeed, and those who do succeed must not be denied the opportunity to elevate their spirit, skills, and desires. In fact, it is those individuals who strive to succeed that move our culture forward.

Considering other people's feelings is important, of course, but to deny, shame, denigrate, ridicule, inhibit or in any way undermine the natural instinct of the human spirit to achieve is nothing less than blind and misguided, if not backward. If someone's feelings are hurt because someone else executes a certain skill or achieves at a higher level, well, that's just life. Get over it; learn from it; grow from it.

Additionally, as my daughter Chandra reminds me, if children lose at some game it would be good for parents to encourage them to keep playing, even if they are not as successful as other children. In fact, they should still play because there is much to be learned, and continuing in the face of defeat can build in children a sense of determination, as well as the courage to try something new. None of us is going to be successful at every game, every task, but what is learned along the way can be parlayed into future experiences, thus helping children grow and become more whole.

The truths outlined in this segment are powerful. They come directly from my lifetime of being a professional martial arts instructor, and are corroborated and enhanced by Chandra's experience of being a highly successful soccer player and parent. Her sister, Christa, would also echo the same truths from her life as a successful CPA and parent. The fact remains that no one rises to an esteemed level in any line of endeavor by holding hands with someone else or working at the level of the mass consciousness. Nor do individuals achieve success by denying their own success in deference to someone else's feelings.

If someone's feelings do get hurt simply because someone else succeeds, then that person needs to get stronger, try harder, work better, sacrifice more, and use the other person's achievement to inspire them. The fact of life is that personal achievement is not a group activity. It is a natural aspect of living and should be honored and applauded, never dishonored, disavowed, or denigrated. That's the natural way of life and it's never going to change. Attempting to make everyone a winner in everything because someone's feelings get hurt is absurd, dangerous, destructive, and anathema to the human spirit.

Teaching Tips

1. Make learning fun! Children love games, and many life lessons can be learned using games as tools in the parenting process.

2. Be creative in creating and playing games. The sky's the limit. Use your imagination.

3. Challenge your children with varying levels of adversity. Don't make games too easy, but do help children to succeed. Succeeding in games teaches confidence through competence and increases a child's self-worth and self-esteem.

4. Do not sacrifice one child's achievement at the expense of another child's feelings. Such action is not only unnatural, it is unfair and unjust.

Managing Opposition

Regarding opposition, which our children will face at some time in their lives, especially if their destinies place them in a leadership position, our children will be benefited if we teach them that they must always do what they feel is right in their hearts. Otherwise, how could they be true to themselves? In this world of duality there will always be an opposing position or point of view to every other position or point of view. How could it be otherwise in a bipolar dimension where the great cosmic pendulum is constantly swinging back and forth, to and fro?

Leaders lead. Abraham Lincoln, arguably the greatest President in United States history, was hated by many people. Yet, he had the strength and courage to do what he believed was right in the face of enormous opposition, and his decisions were proven to be the right thing to do to unify America, although at a heavy cost. Lincoln is revered because he did what he knew was right in his heart. Lincoln is great because he led. He did not follow, he did not buckle under the criticisms of others, nor base his decisions on such criticisms. What tremendous strength there was in Abraham Lincoln!

Likewise, we must also teach our children to not overly concern themselves with the criticisms of others. Look for that which has merit within the criticism but not change their decisions based solely on the criticism. We must also instruct them not to dwell on the negative mindset of other people.

Opposition is an integral aspect of life (as stated), and the purpose of any opposition could well be to simply make our children stronger, more clear in their own position, and determined to do what they think is right. Every cloud does have a silver lining; every opposition has a positive purpose.

A quote from famed British leader and politician Winston Churchill is quite appropriate to this issue:

Kites rise highest against the wind, not with it.

Although ease and comfort are often conditions wished and hoped for in one's life, nothing great ever happened as a result of ease and comfort. Great souls are made under great stress, and great souls always rise to the occasion and to the level of need.

As Buddha said:

There has to be evil so that good can prove its purity above it.

Khalil Gibran, the famous Lebanese-American writer, poet, and artist, accurately noted:

Out of suffering have emerged the strongest souls; the most massive characters are seared with scars.

Winston Churchill stated:

Courage is rightly esteemed the first of human qualities . . . because it is the quality which guarantees all others.

Erica Jong wrote:

> *And the trouble is, if you don't risk anything, you risk even more.*

Because of destiny, we are always perfectly placed. We are never a step ahead or behind where we should be. If we or our children experience opposition, it was predestined, and it has its value and purpose.

As Saint Jagat Singh (20th Century) taught:

> *Our present life is already determined before we are born. What destiny has planned for you will come to pass without any planning on your part. Your destiny will cause you to act and make effort according to its plan.*

Saint Sawan Singh noted:

> *Whatever is happening is all preordained.*

Winston Churchill exhorts:

> *Destiny commands. We must obey!*

Opposition is a natural fact of life. It has purpose. If our destiny calls for there to be opposition in our lives, it will find us. We do not have to go looking for it. If it does find us, it should not be avoided by running away. It should be embraced as a fighter engages his opponent. Opposition is the fire that helps mold the blade of our character, which in turn helps us manage life.

Teaching Tips

1. Teach children that opposition is normal in life and to expect it. Then when they experience it, they will be prepared for it.

2. Provide your child with oppositional experiences through playful means. Have fun through games. It may also be beneficial to explain how the games apply to managing opposition in their lives.

3. If children are concerned about their decision in the face of opposition, recommend to them to ask God for guidance, take action, let Him handle things, and be accepting of whatever happens, knowing that this is His world and He will ultimately do whatever He decides. Teach your children to do their part and then let it go, remaining accepting of the Divine Will.

No Second Chance Guarantee

When we're young we often think life lasts forever and we're indestructible. We also think life will keep giving us chances to "get it right." Maybe we never even consider the chances life is giving us. However we think, one thing is certain – life doesn't always give second chances. Verily, there is *no second chance guarantee.*

It's vital to understand this truth and teach it to our children because if it is not taken to heart, young people, especially teenagers who have an inherent condition of myopia and optimistic indestructibility, may do something which will negatively affect their lives, as well as other people for the remainder of their lives.

What if, for example, a young person is not aware of the potentially catastrophic consequences of consuming alcohol and driving? It is a fact that many lives have been destroyed because of kids drinking and driving and killing. Once a life is destroyed, it can never be brought back. Not only that, but what is to be said about the families, friends, and loved ones not just of the people who died but also of the child who was responsible for the deaths of others? Everyone suffers when there is a death. How many tears will be shed for the remainder of each person's life who was associated with a teenager drinking, driving, and killing? This is one extreme, but nonetheless a very real example of life not giving second chances.

Another example. If children are not educated about the negative aspects of sexual interaction, they could be scarred for life, not just physically, but emotionally, psychologically, and financially. Unfortunately, many movies, television programs, and the media do not address the negative and destructive aspects of sexual interaction among teens and young people. It's almost always about the pleasure and fun of sex but not about the potentially painful, destructive, and regrettable consequences of sex. Therefore, how responsible are those who produce and promote sexual promiscuity?

I'll never forget a talk show interview of a young man who was dying from AIDS. He had engaged in sex one time – one time – and he contracted the deadly disease. His exact words to the audience were, "I was dying to have sex and now I'm dying because I had sex." For him, life never gave him a second chance.

One and done – this is too often the case when people do not take to heart the fact that life doesn't always give second chances. Therefore, children should be taught that *before* they execute an action they need to look ahead to the potential *consequences* of such an action. Once the arrow is loosed from the bow or the bullet from the gun it cannot be brought back.

Another example. What if a parent were to allow his child to spend his youth simply playing around, being undisciplined, indulging in this whim or that whim, neglecting personal and family responsibilities while not paying attention to his education, to developing positive character traits, or to thinking about his future well-being – basically not taking his life seriously? Will the child one day look back and ask why his life is in such shambles, all the time lamenting that there are no more chances for him to make a better life for himself because he spent his youth frivolously and foolishly? Will the destructive qualities of bitterness, anger, and resentment set in? If the time of youth is wasted, what will the time of adulthood bring?

And how will the parent feel if his child experiences such a life? Guilty? Shameful? Unconcerned?

The fact is, life is serious business right from the start. It's okay to have fun in life but not at the expense of the quality of life. If a child misses the opportunity of doing well in school, for example, he may never get the chance to create the foundation that a positive educational experience offers. There is no rallying around a dilly-dallying past. It is a wise parent who teaches his children their responsibility of doing their best in school in order to create a foundation that will serve and support them when they become adults and, potentially, parents.

Following are some excellent quotations for consideration.

> *For of all sad words of tongue or pen, the saddest are these, it might have been* (John Greenleaf Whittier, "Maud Muller").

> *I will prepare and some day my chance will come* (Abraham Lincoln).

> *It is not often that a man can make opportunities for himself, but he can put himself in such shape that when or if the opportunities come he is ready* (Theodore Roosevelt).

> *My country owes me nothing. It gave me, as it gives every boy and girl, a chance. It gave me schooling, independence of action, opportunity for service and honor* (Herbert Hoover).

Unfortunately, there seems to be far more opportunity out there than ability . . . We should remember that good fortune often happens when opportunity meets with preparation (Thomas Edison).

How much I missed, simply because I was afraid of missing it (Paulo Coelho).

Teaching Tips

1. Parents need to be vigilant in educating children that life doesn't always give second chances. This is especially true if the decisions have major negative risks, especially to others.

2. An excellent teaching technique for parents is that when their children have to make a difficult choice, the parents should have the children envision the potential outcomes of such a choice. Are there dangers to oneself? Dangers to others? What are the inherent risks of the choice? What are the opportunities, potentials, liabilities? What are the up sides and the down sides? When children are taught to take time and reflect on potential consequences ahead of their choices, their chances of making better choices are enhanced.

No Whining

To help children grow strong and stable there needs to be a *Zero Whining* policy in the family. Whining, wailing, whimpering, bemoaning, grumbling, and griping do not make children strong, self-assured, whole, confident, noble, and dignified as they grow into adulthood. Babies whine. Mature adults do not.

Everyone in life has problems, troubles, challenges, heartaches, and heartbreaks. Everyone has their tales of woe to tell. So why tell them? Nobody really wants to hear about someone else's problems anyway because they have their own to deal with.

Of course whining and wailing often make us feel better in the moment, but they undermine our strength and nobility. They serve no substantive purpose. They don't help us grow or mature. Rather, they keep us from growing, maturing, and evolving into a more worthy and substantive individual. Whining and whimpering make us look small, not tall.

If you're an athletic coach, you know the truth of this principle. If a child starts complaining or whining on a football, hockey, basketball, baseball, soccer, rugby, or any other team, the child will have a rude awakening, which will not be a joyful experience. As a professional martial arts instructor and father, I never allowed such destructive behavior in my students or children. Our job as parents is, in part, to make our children strong. They will never be strong if we teach them to be weak by enabling their wailing and whining. Therefore, it's wise to teach children as soon as possible to, as Saint Kabir would say, *Keep your mouth shut and suffer all in silence.*

Teaching Tips

1. Set the rule in the household – *No Whining Allowed.* Do it as soon as children have an understanding of language. When they do whine, and they will as all children do, tell them, "No whining allowed." Keep reinforcing the rule until they understand. They won't appreciate it until they get older and see other people whining, and then they'll be able to compare and contrast their own behavior to that of others. Too, they'll see the positive results in themselves and be grateful to you as the parent for teaching them to be courageous, strong, whole, and whining/whimpering free.

2. Point out to children as they grow examples of people who do not complain, whine, or whimper. Explain to them how noble, courageous, and dignified such individuals are. This method is much preferred to pointing out whiners and complainers. It's always best to use the positive approach rather than the negative.

3. Perhaps the most important teaching tip is for us parents not to whine, whimper, or complain. After all, if we whine, how could we possibly have any credibility in preaching to our children to not whine. Parenting is not about preaching, it's about guiding and leading . . . by example.

Parental Sovereignty of Children

In this socialistic age there exists an idea being promoted by some individuals and college professors that our children are really not our own, that they belong to the state, not the parents, and that children would be better cared for by the government – dictating what the children learn, what they eat or don't eat, mandated immunizations, and so forth.

This concept of the state or government taking responsibility for raising and guiding our children is referred to as the *social collective*. Its basis is that the government knows better how to raise, educate, guide, and teach our children than we parents do. If you are unfamiliar with this concept, I would suggest doing your own research and keeping your parental ears close to the ground.

Frankly, from my point of view, this is not only wrong but dangerous. Children are biologically tied to their parents, not to a government, and we parents, for the most part, are doing a fine job. We don't need government bureaucrats telling us how to raise our children, and if we are loving, caring, responsible parents the thought of abdicating our parental rights to some bureaucratic institution is irrefutably incomprehensible, if not laughable.

Our children are *our* children. They do not belong to someone or something else. Such concepts violate basic laws of Nature. To throw all children into one socialistic pot is to deny them the natural care they would get from their biological parents. Occasionally, some children may need care by a social institution, but government is not the primary answer. Private institutions, church organizations, and other such entities can step in to help in such cases. People are generous. Governments are gluttonous. Parents, in the main, know best. Governments have no business involving themselves in the raising of our children except in rare cases.

A simple parenting question: "Why would any rational, reasonable, and responsible parents want someone else or some social collective raising their children?" Honestly, do you want someone else's values creating the foundation for your children? Would you trust someone else to care for your children more than you, to look after and ensure their highest and best good more than you?

Having a government take charge of its nation's children is not only dumbing down the God-given natural duty of parenting, but it also dumbs down children, indoctrinating them into thinking the state knows best and is much wiser and more capable than individual parents. Placing any bureaucratic institution in charge of raising children not only destroys the natural concept of the family, but destroys parental responsibility and individuality, denuding parents not only of their parental rights but their parental obligations.

If two adults agree to have a child or children, they become primarily responsible for raising their children, and they must own up to such a commitment. Having some government-mandated social collective do the natural parent's job lets the parents off the hook, destroying individual responsibility and accountability, thus creating weakness en masse.

Having and raising children is serious business. It is not child's play, and should never be passed off as a football, baseball, basketball, or hockey puck is passed off to a teammate in some game. Children are not playthings, and parenting is not a game. Children deserve to be honored, respected, and cared for by their natural parents. This is real life.

Teaching Tips

1. Be ever vigilant as a parent in your duties and responsibilities of having children and raising them yourself. Do not abdicate parental duties to some government or social collective. Give your children the opportunity to be loved and nurtured by their own biological parents. They deserve no less.

2. Pay attention to what others are saying and speak up against any thought or action that seeks to make the raising of children a government-mandated function.

3. Obviously, this world has become socially based with a myriad of social websites and platforms such as Facebook, Twitter, and so forth. Independence, it would seem, is giving way to dependence. It would be unwise to allow the growth of this social energy to overpower or subjugate the natural process of the parent/child relationship.

4. Know that as a parent you have a natural God-given sovereignty and responsibility to raise your children and no argument to the contrary will ever be valid in the main.

Pity-Pot Poison

Nothing is more poisonous to our sense of wholeness than feeling sorry for ourselves. Self-pity destroys. It doesn't have to be voiced. It can be silent. If it is silent, it becomes a silent killer. As parents, if we wish our children to be whole, balanced, and productive as they grow and mature, we can not allow them to sit on their pity-pots and feel sorry for themselves.

Famous English novelist, poet, and playwright D. H. Lawrence beautifully encapsulates the concept of self-pity:

> *I never saw a wild thing sorry for itself. A small bird will drop frozen dead from a bough without ever having felt sorry for itself.*

American icon and author Helen Keller observes:

> *Self-pity is our worst enemy and if we yield to it, we can never do anything wise in this world.*

Millicent Fenwick, an American fashion editor, politician, and diplomat of the 20th Century states:

> *Never feel self-pity, the most destructive emotion there is. How awful to be caught up in the terrible squirrel cage of self.*

Teaching Tips

1. Instill in your children that feeling sorry for oneself is a weakness of character. There is nothing positive, strong, noble, great, or grand in negative self-indulgence. Self-pity is an egregiously limiting and destructive quality that serves no useful purpose.

2. Sit with your children and help them count their blessings. Let them cultivate a sense of gratitude for everything they have – from the smallest and most insignificant to the largest and most significant. Each of us has more to be grateful for than we know. By making a habit of counting our blessings we overcome a sense of self-pity and move into a nobler state of mind and consciousness.

3. Teach your children the powerful two-word phrase, *Thank You*. This will help keep them developing the virtue of humility, which in turn will help them avoid the equally destructive quality of entitlement. Factually, no one is entitled to anything in life, and by constantly expressing the words *Thank You*, we teach our children to acknowledge our appreciation of life itself, even in the most minute of ways.

4. If by chance we parents are having our own bout with self-pity, let us at least hide somewhere where our children cannot see us. It does them no good. And if we are ourselves

succumbing to a pity-pot moment, let us, too, start counting our blessings as we cleanse ourselves of its poison.

5. Treat being on the pity-pot like whining. Establish a zero tolerance policy for both because both are limiting, destructive, ignoble.

Sticks And Stones

Whatever happened to *Sticks and stones may break my bones but words can never hurt me*? Incredibly, it seems as though many people today fall apart at the mere whisper of someone's verbal mutterings and utterings directed toward them. And to make matters worse, the person who believes he has been slighted and hurt demands an apology.

Such hypersensitivity in being hurt by what someone says is not conducive to well-balanced, whole, happy, stable children or adults. Words are simply vocal utterances. The only power they have is the power we give them. Otherwise, words are impotent. They can't hurt us at all. Yet, we allow them to hurt us. We let their power overpower us, sending a message that we are powerless. Really?

Reflect for a moment on what it says about us when we overreact to something someone says, especially about us. It says we are not fully integrated as an individual, that we have abdicated our personal power and given that power to someone else. It says that others are in control of us and we are not in control of ourselves. It says we are so weak that we allow simple words – words – to affect us negatively. It says we, therefore, need to get stronger, to be more whole, to be more balanced and centered.

Rather than reacting negatively to derisive statements made toward us, which are impossible to stop, we need to realize the problem is not with us but with the individual uttering such thoughts. Frankly, we need to feel sorry for such souls and have pity for them, thus being proactive and not reactive.

From apple trees we get apples. From orange trees we get oranges. From loving, kind, caring, positive people we get loving, kind, caring, positive thoughts. Antithetically, from unloving, unkind, uncaring, negative people we get unloving, unkind, uncaring, negative thoughts.

Consider the source. Would we be upset by a worm's malicious vituperations directed toward us? Of course not. So don't empower the worm. Low-level people generate low-level thoughts. High-level people generate high-level thoughts. When we succumb to being hurt by low-level thoughts and the misguided souls uttering them, we not only degrade ourselves but we empower those who voice such negativity. In doing so, we are actually supporting such negativity. We need to maintain the high ground and ignore such emptiness.

And why demand apologies from such people? Not only do we disempower ourselves by allowing someone's words to hurt us, we actually empower the people uttering verbal assaults by acknowledging their negativity and power over us, which we bequeath to them by acting hurt. By not demanding any apology we simply dismiss the worm and maintain our own power and control.

The reality is that no one can hurt us unless we allow ourselves to be hurt. Words are words. That's all. The only power they have is the power we give them. To allow someone's words to hurt us is to abdicate our own personal power, to empower others, and support their negative mindset. This is weakness, not strength. If we are to teach our children to be strong, whole, and confident, they need to learn how not to let someone's else words hurt them. The weakness is in those who speak negatively, not us. We only become weak when we acknowledge such negativity and react to it.

Teaching Tips

1. Teach your children to consider the source of any negative comments directed toward them. Use the "from apples we get apples" analogy. Positive people don't emit negative comments toward others, and we should not let our children be affected by such negative energies.

2. We need to teach our children not to think negatively about those who are negative, but rather to have pity and sympathy for such souls. They are the ones who are weak and suffering, and their weakness and negativity is simply an expression of that suffering.

3. Instruct children to ignore the derisive comments from others and keep moving forward, and certainly to not demand any apologies, which only empowers the otherwise powerless.

4. Instill in children a realization of their own power and not to give that power away by allowing someone else's negativity to hurt them and thus disempower them.

5. Words are not bombs or bullets. They're vocal utterances. That's all. They have no intrinsic destructive capability unless we give it to them. Don't give it to them.

6. *Don't empower the worm.*

Tender Love Versus Tough Love

Love is absolutely essential in the process of raising children. But how is love defined? By soft kisses, tender hugs, a constant flow of endearing statements and "I love yous?" Or is it defined by establishing and enforcing a fair but strict set of standards, guidelines, and restrictions? Is loving our children giving them everything they desire, or balancing their needs with their wants?

My personal viewpoint is that loving our children should be both tender and tough. Excessive tenderness makes them weak and dependent. Excessive toughness makes them wary, bitter, and hard. As parents, we need to find a balance point between *tender* and *tough*. As always, *balance is primary*.

The principle of *Tender and Tough* should begin earlier than later. This is because the greatest percentage of the structural foundation of children occurs within the first few years of life. This may sound harsh but it really isn't. *Tough* simply means not being overly soft, which is very easy to do with small children because we make the mistake of thinking they're totally helpless. This may be true from a physical standpoint but not from a mental one. Our dear little children, even at ages one and two, are oftentimes smarter than we think.

For example, when children cry is their crying legitimate or manipulative? If children are in physical pain that certainly needs to be addressed. But don't think for a second that our little babes are beyond the skill of manipulation because they're not. There is a distinct difference between real tears and crocodile tears, and children can often be pros when playing the role of the crocodile. If we parents fall prey to such acting, we will not strengthen our children but actually weaken them through our enabling.

Manipulative tears often start to flow when children do not get what they want. They start crying, perhaps screaming and throwing temper tantrums. If we parents buckle at such thespian expression because we want to have a "loving" heart and give them what their vituperations demand, we lose; they lose.

Giving in to our children's demands is not loving them. It's crippling them, and we may not even be aware of it. The result, if we don't change our methods and continue to support their tantrums and reinforce their negative behavior, is that our children will become spoiled and entitled, and it will be our fault. If we extrapolate this behavior, we will see that our spoiled and entitled little children will grow to be spoiled and entitled adults.

Tough love is love that understands this principle of child manipulation and does not fall prey to it. Make no mistake – children are very smart, and they know how to get to their parents, push their buttons, and get what they (the children) want. Tough love stops them in their tracks and says . . .

> *No. I will not give in to your temper tantrums. I will not cripple you. I will not be an enabler or promoter of your bad behavior. I will truly love you and make you strong, not weak. I will teach you that such negative behavior is not in your highest and best good. You may not know this at this time of your life, but I do, and as a parent I will do what is in your ultimate best interest.*

Thus, loving children does not mean to allow them to throw temper tantrums that go unchallenged and undisciplined. Unchecked behaviors send a clear message to children that they are free to do whatever they want because there will be no reprisals, no consequences, no price to pay. When this happens they become stronger and parents become weaker. Children will not take parents seriously, nor will they respect them. In effect, the children control the parents. Not good. Parents must never relinquish the responsibility to take control of their offspring. As children grow and become responsible for their actions then, yes, control should be lessened accordingly.

So how do we parents not cave in to our children's negative behaviors? First, by recognizing that as parents we are our children's leaders. They are not our leaders. Second, by being stronger than our children. Third, by learning to say "no" and being consistent in our disciplinary actions.

This gives rise to the subject of discipline. Discipline has been given a bad name. Discipline is not a bad thing. In fact it is a critical aspect of one's personal character and success in life. It is especially important when raising children. But because discipline has been given a bad name, parents often think they should never discipline their children and that loving them is giving them everything they desire.

This is obvious through a simple glimpse of today's society. There are a great number of spoiled and entitled adults who truly believe the world owes them a comfortable life, and when they don't get it, they throw adult-sized temper tantrums, threaten those who don't give them what they want, denigrate them, call them names, and do all they can to destroy them in order to get their way. Such adults are really just children who never grew up. Just because a person is accompanied by an adult body does not mean he or she exhibits adult behavior. How did such people get this way? Certainly one explanation is that they were not the recipients of *tough love*. Maybe they had no love at all.

Basically, *tough love* is being able to say "no" when necessary, and being able to discipline when necessary, and discipline there must be if we want the best for our children.

Teaching Tips

1. Learn to say "no" and mean it. Be consistent. Don't waffle.

2. Be careful what you say, and if you are not willing to follow through on your disciplinary threat, don't say it. Think before you act. For example, if you tell your misbehaving child he will have a time out against the wall if he continues his bad behavior, then make sure you follow through and put him in a time out if he misbehaves again. By making your actions equal your words, he will get the message. However, if you don't follow through, he will learn your words are simply idle threats and he will continue to misbehave. This lack of backing up one's threats is all too common in parenting. The result is continuing bad behavior by the child and a disrespecting of you and your parental authority.

3. When you discipline a child make sure you explain to him why he is being disciplined. This not only takes the sting out of his punishment but lets him know what lines not to cross in the future, thus enabling him to manage his life and relationship with you better. Explanations create guidelines for behavior.

4. Remember, there's nothing wrong in disciplining your child. Discipline is a natural act of nature. Animals discipline their young. Why should man think differently?

5. Discipline should be positive and consistent, never negative or inconsistent. Kids not only appreciate discipline (because it establishes boundaries for them) they need it. Without discipline children grow to be unruly, lost, and often lead scraggly, substanceless lives.

6. Don't buckle under your child's protestations. Parental disciplinary measures can become a battle of wills between child and parent. Parents must win this battle of wills. This means they must endure and not give in to temper tantrums and other acts of adolescent outrage and misbehavior.

The Five Needs of Children

There are many things children need. As parents we all have our own lists. Five of a child's most basic needs from my personal point of view are: love, structure, guidance, discipline, attention. These can be easily remembered by their letters: L-S-G-D-A.

Love

The first need of children has to be love. Having love in one's life and being loved will balance so many problems and issues that children may have otherwise. There are of course many definitions, expressions, and levels of love.

My expression of love for my children is to make sure they know that as a father I am always there for them, will never abandon them, and that I will care for and support them in their lives. I believe in doing for my children that which is in their highest and best good. My fatherly/parental duty is also to prepare them for an adult life – to be responsible, independent, strong, loving, and free.

Structure

No building can stand without a structure, a foundation. Likewise, a child's life cannot stand without a structure, a foundation. From my point of view, a substantive foundation is one designed with boundaries, rules, and regulations wrapped in a loving blanket of protective arms with supportive hands that continually nudge the child up the ladder of independence, competence, confidence, self-esteem, strength, responsibility, wholeness, and self-realization.

Obviously, all parents will have their own blueprint for creating a foundation for their children. The point to be made is that having a viable structure for children as they grow is vital to ensure they have a meaningful and substantive adult life.

The concept of "structure" is composed of sub-structures such as rules to be followed at home, rules for social interaction with adults, behavioral patterns, managing money, etc. All structures (primary or secondary) have multiple purposes for children. They act as protective walls during the most critical years of their lives. Structures, serving as an anchor, stabilize children and keep them from being washed away in the tides of life or blown away by the often-turbulent world winds of youth. And, as stated, structures create a critical foundation upon which the rest of the life rests.

Guidance

What do I do? Where do I go? Children deserve answers to these questions, and as parents who want the best for our children, it is incumbent upon us to guide them, not simply give birth to them and abandon them to the whims of the world while we pursue our own self interests.

Parents are leaders, guides. Children are too young to know how to navigate their life's journey. That's where we come in. Part of our parenting role is to be a travel guide during their early years, to show them the way, revealing the best paths to a fulfilling life while avoiding the pitfalls, dead ends, and quicksand pits along the journey.

Unfortunately, many children are left to figure out everything on their own while their parents are off doing their thing, obviously oblivious to their primary role of caring for the children they brought into the world. Yet, the fact is that once we have children, our personal lives as parents should take a backseat to raising our children. After we've done our job and our kids transition into adult life, then we can resume our personal interests on a fuller scale.

One excellent tool for guiding children, especially during their formative years which establish the trunk of the tree of their lives, is for parents to understand the destinies of their children. An excellent source parents can use during this process of child guidance is *Parenting Wisdom for the 21st Century – Raising Your Children By Their Numbers To Achieve Their Highest Potential* (available at RichardKing.net and online bookstores).

Discipline

Discipline keeps children from straying beyond the boundaries of safety. It works hand-in-hand with the concept of *structure*, for discipline is personal structure.

It is discipline, parentally imposed in the early life of a child and becoming self-imposed as he or she matures, that helps ensure a life of substance, success, fulfillment, safety, security, happiness. If a working sense of discipline is not established in childhood, it will be extremely difficult to cultivate it later on, creating potential problems.

The famous Greek mathematician, scientist, and philosopher Pythagoras stated:

No man is free who cannot control himself.

How true is this statement! We think that freedom is being able to do whatever we want when we want. The truth, however, is that unrestrained actions and behaviors don't lead to freedom but slavery.

For example, if a person becomes involved in recreational drug usage because he thinks he's free, he may well soon discover that his "freedom" resulted in an addiction to the very object he freely pursued. Had he learned the critically valuable virtue of discipline, with its by-product of self-control, he would never have succumbed to drugs and the living hell they create.

As we parent our children, it is important to teach them discipline, to restrain their desires relating to those actions which can hurt, maim, or destroy their lives. So many children today run after the pleasures of the world, ignorant of the massive pain they bring. Our job as parents should be to train our children in the art of discipline so they can avoid the tragic results of an undisciplined life.

Attention

Children could have all the external factors supporting them – food, shelter, clothing, money – but nothing is more critical than personal, loving attention from their parents. If we parents do not give our children the attention they deserve, where then will they get it? Television? Friends? Internet? Social media? Diabolic miscreants pandering to their need for love and attention?

Children need parental attention first and foremost. This can be in many forms. Simply hanging out with them, talking with them, going for walks together, watching television, doing projects, sharing life's experiences, and having dinner together are all ways in which we parents can give attention to our children.

Perhaps the most important thing regarding attention is simply the giving of our *time* to our children. What could be more powerful? Money? Gifts? Music lessons? No. Nothing is more valuable than giving attention through time. Why? Because it is the most personal. Giving our children time shows we care about them, that we love them, value them, and want to nurture them. Simply giving them money or things sends a message that we don't have time for them, so we placate them with something other than us. However, when we give our children attention by giving them our time, we all win, and the children grow up with a greater sense of parental love.

Love, structure, guidance, discipline, and attention (L-S-G-D-A): these are the five basic needs of children, at least in my opinion. They cover a lot of parenting ground, and they're important. They help our children grow into balanced, whole, substantive adults, and they give us, as parents, a simple, direct, and easy format to follow in raising them. L-S-G-D-A – five simple letters that can have a powerful effect on parents and children alike.

Teaching Tips

1. Memorize the L-S-G-D-A format and consider it a powerful formula in the process of parenting. Review it daily and ask yourself if you are using it . . . daily. It won't work unless you work it.

2. None of us is a perfect parent. We should see ourselves as a work in progress and keep working to improve our parenting skills through the L-S-G-D-A formula.

3. Talking is one thing, doing is another. In giving our children the basic needs they crave and deserve, we should *do*, not just talk. Are you *doing*?

4. Giving *time* to our children is critical to their wholeness. It lets them know we care about them, and that we're willing to sacrifice our personal interests for them. What could be more important to a parent than raising children who are balanced and whole? Time goes by very quickly, and the last thing we want as loving parents is to look back after our children are grown and gone, and realize we did not give them enough of our time, our love, our attention, and have to live with that burden for the rest of our lives.

The Four Cornerstones Of A Substantive Life

Building a life, like building anything else, begins with a foundation. In general terms, the stronger the foundation the stronger the building; the weaker the foundation the weaker the building. Exempt a natural catastrophe, structures built on rock or solid ground can expect a substantive life, but structures built on sand are doomed from the beginning.

As parents, what kind of foundation will we create for our children? Have we even considered the concept of creating a foundation for them, let alone a strong one? And if we have considered creating a foundation, what will its components be?

One foundational child-raising blueprint is composed of four solid cornerstones of life:

1. Character
2. Balance
3. Ticker
4. Independence

Character

Character is the primary cornerstone of every life that is decent, good, meaningful, and substantive. If one's character is deficient, the life will also be deficient. Character precedes prowess; character precedes wealth; character precedes celebrity; character precedes popularity; character precedes social status, rank, peer pressure, and political position; character precedes worldly achievement; character precedes spiritual ascent. The redundancy here is by design. Character precedes everything, and if character is subordinated to anything, the life lived, regardless of its worldly success, will be meaningless and will wash away like sand beset with ocean waves. Character is that critical to a truly successful life. If there is no character, what is there?

Building character is not easy. It demands much – persistence, patience, sacrifice, determination, discipline, self-control, courage, desire, and an iron will not to buckle under the pressures of the lures of worldly riches, power, celebrity, social status, and all things that glitter with material magnetism.

This is not to say that success, wealth, celebrity, etc., are negative, but it is to say that they become negative *if* they are sacrificed at the expense of one's character. And this is the rub – do we teach our children to focus on the ephemeral or eternal aspects of life? Material things are not eternal. Our spirit, our soul, is eternal. It is pure energy and cannot be destroyed, whereas material things can. Therefore, placing the material before the spiritual is a losing proposition. This is why character – a function of the spirit – precedes everything. Once character is lost, all is lost.

Balance

Life runs smoothly when its components are in balance. It becomes very rocky when its components are out of balance. Without question, if our children are to have a chance of a substantive, meaningful, fulfilling, and successful life, we must teach them to maintain balance in all areas of their lives. Life is difficult enough when we do everything right, but when any aspect gets out of balance, there will be complications. For a more thorough treatment of balance, read the section *Balance Is Primary*.

Ticker

Ticker means having a kind and tender heart. It is an expression of love and compassion for all life. Having *ticker* anchors our character in spiritual energy. Too often in life we become saturated with worldly accomplishment and self-aggrandizement. Our success and notoriety make us blind to the sufferings of others. Yet, it is the warmth of our caring that sets us apart and makes us special.

Think back to the people in your life who had the greatest impact on you. Was it the richest individual you've ever known? A famous celebrity? A sports hero? Movie star? Priest? Reverend? Professor? Teacher? My bet is that for most people the person they remember most in their lives was the one who had *ticker*, who loved and supported them, who made them feel warm and comfortable, who acknowledged them for who they were and who encouraged them to be all they could be.

Yet, how common are people who truly exude *ticker*, whether they're family members, team members, teachers, professors, doctors, nurses, lawyers, bankers, friends, acquaintances, or the clerk in the corner store? Compare the number of people in life who have *ticker* with those individuals who criticize, patronize, ridicule, vilify, discount, dismiss, denounce, deprecate, denigrate, and depreciate. The former group is extremely rare; the latter group is the norm, unfortunately.

This simple observation reveals how important *ticker* is when living a substantive life. What good is it to be rich when we're vilified, if being famous only brings scorn, if being powerful only creates distrust?

It is important for children, especially those who choose to excel, to learn this critical principle of *ticker*, of having a kind and tender heart, of acknowledging others whose destiny may not bring them worldly success, but whose soul is equal to theirs. Arguably, more than any other trait it is *ticker* that makes a person successful and substantive because it is so very rare. For more, read the section *First Comes Ticker*.

Independence

There is nothing more critical to survival than a sense of independence. Being able to stand alone, think alone, act alone – in spite of obstacles, challenges, and hardships – is a fundamental cornerstone of a substantive life.

Humans are, by nature, social. They like to interact and belong to groups and communities. Yet, the bottom line of individual life is that each of us is responsible for ourself. After we reach the age of maturity (generally accepted as eighteen), we are responsible for our lives. We can remonstrate, demonstrate, protest, argue, strike, bemoan our lot in life, point fingers, and claim that another person or body of individuals is responsible for us but such reasoning just won't fly. Each of us is responsible for our self in spite of any argument to the contrary. This subject of independence is fully treated in the sections *Your Life, Your Responsibility* and *You're On Your Own*.

Everyone's destiny is different. Some individuals may have a life of extreme social interaction. This would be noted by the amalgam of social numbers in their King's Numerology chart (2-4-6-8). Other individuals may have a destiny filled with the numerical energies of being solo, free, and solitary (1-5-7). These people would be intrinsically more independent than those with social numbers, but this does not preclude anyone from being responsible for his or her own life. (For more on the relationship between one's numbers and destiny, read the companion work to this book, *Parenting Wisdom For The 21st Century – Raising Your Children By Their Numbers To Achieve Their Highest Potential*).

One of the major advantages of teaching our children to be independent is that they will not think of themselves as helpless, dependent, entitled, or spoiled. They will be able to take charge of their lives and avoid the chains of dependency and the shackles of entitlement. Should they become parents, they will be positive role models for their own children.

If we want our children to be strong and whole, teaching them to be independent should be a primary lesson we should reinforce in them as they mature and move into the world of adulthood.

These four important and critical cornerstones for creating a substantive life – character, balance, ticker, and independence – are a formidable force in the parenting process. Yet, there is still one more "stone" to be addressed – the *Capstone*.

The Capstone

The *Capstone* is the "stone" that sits atop the structure created by the four cornerstones for all to see. The *capstone* is the crowing achievement or goal of the cornerstones supporting it.

What do we want the capstone of our children's lives to be? Certainly, the cornerstones will play a major role in this determination. Whatever the crowning achievement is, if a child is raised with the fundamental and foundational principles of character, balance, ticker, and independence, the radiance of the capstone will be substantial.

Teaching Tips

1. Never allow children to lose sight of the four cornerstones that help create a substantive life: character, balance, ticker, and independence. Teach these principles, reinforce them whenever and wherever possible as children grow and, hopefully, mature into whole, substantive, and responsible adults.

The Process Is The Product

When any individual (adult or child) is aspiring toward a goal, the goal is often considered the product – the valued reward for the hard work, effort, and excellence needed to achieve the goal, i.e., the product. Such *product rewards* may be a certain amount of money, a championship title in a sport, a level of educational achievement, rising to become the president of a company or corporation, climbing to the top of a mountain, winning an Olympic Gold Medal and on and on. The list of *product rewards* is endless. Such rewards have merit, of course, but are they the only measure of success? Is there no other measure of success than what one gains at the end of the struggle? Are things, titles, trophies, etc., the only treasures of achievement?

What often happens when individuals struggle for years to achieve a goal and they fail? Disappointment and depression are natural feelings in such cases, but too often the real gift, the real *product reward*, is overlooked and not given any value whatsoever. Upon deeper reflection, whether one "succeeds" or not, is the thing achieved really the product, the reward, the gift for the struggle? Or is the *process* the real product, the real gift, the real reward?

In martial arts training there are many levels of achievement, the Black Belt being the most sought after. But does this mean that an individual who does not achieve a black belt ranking has not succeeded? Even if a legitimate black belt ranking from a legitimate school is achieved, is that the only thing recognized as the end product? As a professional lifetime martial arts instructor I can say with absolute certainty, "no." The achievement of any belt level is worthy of recognition because in the final analysis, *the process is the product*, not the belt.

Why is the process the product? The answer is that in the effort to achieve a goal, the gift that will endure the most is the *process* of achieving that goal. Just think of all the wonderful attributes and skills acquired in the process of achievement – enormous amounts of energy, effort, time, sweat, study, sacrifice, dedication, devotion, determination, discipline, concentration, commitment, consistency, courage, strength, adjustment, adaptation, pain, hurt, flexibility, persistence, resilience, and a relentless desire to succeed. These are great gifts.

It is the development of these universal attributes of the struggle to achieve that is the real trophy, the real reward, the real attainment. Such virtues comprise the energetic fabric of our character, and it is these virtues that become a part of us forever, even when we move on after this life.

The composite of our energy and character that we develop in this life will go with us into the next phase of our life journey. Things, titles, trophies will not. So of what real value do such things ultimately have? The answer is *none*. What lives in perpetuity are those virtues we learn and make a part of us while alive because they *will* go with us in the end. Therefore, in truth, *the process is the product* in any effort to achieve, whether or not some thing, title, or trophy is gained.

So do we teach our children not to try for the gold ring? No, because were we to do that, they would not expend the effort, time, discipline, devotion, etc., to achieve the end. They would ignore the process which is, in the final analysis, the great and enduring product.

If they do gain the gold ring, fine, but if they do not, it does not mean they have failed, and we should remind them that just because they don't finish in first place they haven't failed. They have succeeded, maybe not to the level they desired, but they have succeeded nonetheless. They have developed traits in themselves that create a foundation of life and living that will be with them forever. In fact, given the choice of some worldly symbol of achievement or the development of one's character, the latter is by far the more important. When our children understand this, they will achieve a salutary state of balance, placing the subject of achievement in its proper perspective. They will become wise, mature, substantive.

Teaching Tips

1. Do encourage children to achieve. As this book teaches, to have a high life you have to have a high bar. However, do explain to them that just because they may not achieve the worldly goals they desire does not mean they have failed. Remind them of the enormous success they have achieved during the process of striving to achieve. Teach them how to compare and contrast virtues gained versus things gained. Explain to them the substantive value of the virtues acquired in the process of attainment which create the foundation of their entire lives going forward. Do not allow them to think they failed just because their goals did not meet their expectations. This said, keep encouraging them to continue to achieve because the continuation will further strengthen them.

2. Remembering that *the process is the product* is just as important for us parents as it is for our children, perhaps more so. How many times has each of us struggled to achieve, not achieved the goal we were seeking, become discouraged and depressed, and overlooked the intrinsic gift of the *process*? Has such activity helped us or hindered us? I think there's a lot to gain by reflecting on how we have managed the successes and failures of our lives.

The Temptations of S.A.D.

This is a very challenging time for parents and children. So much is moving so fast, and not all of it is wholeness-engendering, positive, or conducive to a happy, substantive life. The world's population is ever-expanding, ideologies are clashing, terrorism is extant, the potential of nuclear war looms large with the proliferation of nuclear-armed countries, reason has been overpowered by emotion, and ethical conduct and moral values are constantly under attack.

The purity of a child's innocence is also being assaulted from an early age. Three of the greatest temptations, which are potential destroyers of children and their lives, can be placed in the acronym S.A.D., which stands for sex, alcohol, and drugs (S.A.D.).

Life is hard enough if we do everything right, or at least try to do everything right. But when the reckless and misguided involvement of sex, alcohol, and drugs enters the life equation, there cannot be a positive outcome. Life doesn't always give second chances, and one major mistake with any of these three pleasure-based opiates (PBOs) could change a life forever in a very sad and tragic way.

S.A.D.s are the seducers of mankind. Because of their pleasure-oriented composition they exist as prodigious temptations for young people. It does not help that multiple elements of our adult society promote these PBOs shamelessly and selflessly, giving the diabolic impression that their consumption is appropriate, hip, and cool. S.A.D.s are nothing of the sort, and if the downside of their usage is not taught and exposed they will continue to be great provocative destroyers, not just of children but mankind as well.

Without even considering the negative effect PBOs have on one's spiritual existence, the worldly consequences are bad enough. Following are a few personal observations.

Sex

Sexual energies are extremely powerful, and promiscuous sexual conduct is powerfully dangerous, even detrimental. Where has the misuse of sexual energy not damaged or destroyed people in all walks of life throughout the history of mankind? As 15th/16th Century Saint Ravidas declares:

> *The affliction of lust is the foremost trap of the world.*

Saint Kabir, also a 15th/16th Saint, states:

> *Sex indulgence is the lowest of human activities. That men should be at all proud of it surpasses understanding.*

Yet, our culture continues to promote and elevate sex as something of which to be proud. Sex is a normal biological function. However, to glorify it on an alter of fame, fortune, and success is beyond the pale of human edification and, furthermore, it's a rather deplorable marker of measurement on the scale of human spirituality. To promote as highest that which is lowest does not bode well for human evolution and maturity.

However, our culture is what it is, and though the culture may one day shift, in the meantime we parents would be wise to educate our children as to the dangers of inappropriate sexual behavior, something which is never done by those who use sex as a marketing tactic to increase the size of their coffers.

The dangers associated with sex are real and extensive. How many lives have been permanently damaged, even destroyed, by any one of a plethora of sexually transmitted diseases (STDs)? How many babies in the womb have been murdered through abortion because, although people engage in sex for their pleasure, some of them refuse to accept responsibility for their actions, basically placing their personal pleasure and comfort before the sanctity of life itself? How can such action possibly be defended with any modicum of spirituality, humanity, sanity, intelligence, or reason?

Just for the record, abortion is not a political issue, it is a life issue transcending human choice and its addiction to pleasure. If an individual is wise, he or she will take to heart the reality of cause and effect, sowing and reaping, karma. It is an inescapable and immutable law of this creation that what we place onto the circle of life will, without fail, circle back to encircle us. In other words, those who destroy life will have their lives destroyed. Those who abort babies will themselves eventually be aborted. As 17th/18th Century Saint Dariya of Bihar exclaims:

> *The sower of the poison cannot but be engulfed in the poison.*

Saint Ravidas warns:

> *The fruit of action unfailing overtakes the doer.*

Saint Charan Singh warns:

If we kill we will be killed. We should never forget that.

Thus, as parents we would be wise to instruct our children in the dangers of sex. Society, the media, entertainment industry, and all those entities who make money through the promotion of sex will never address the downside of sex and its dangers. Such is the dark power of money. If we want our children to live as healthy a life as possible, as substantive a life as possible, as problem-free a life as possible, then we must educate our young. After all, our children are our responsibility, not someone else's.

Alcohol

As socially and universally popular and acceptable as the consumption of alcohol is, it is still a drug and a poison. It is also a destroyer. Like inappropriate and careless sexual conduct, alcohol has been responsible for untold misery, pain, suffering, sorrow, tragedy, and death. A moment of simple, mature, and thoughtful reflection will bring to light the insidious nature of this all-too-accepted universal pleasure-based opiate.

Of course, like peddlers of sex, peddlers of alcohol will not address this aspect of their product. They will defend it, but defend it successfully they cannot, nor can they be cleansed of their actions by simply telling people to drink responsibly. Words cannot exonerate people from their actions, however deflective such statements appear to be on the surface. How can promoting poison and its consumption be at all responsible? Rather, it is reprehensible. Poisons kill people. Alcohol kills people. Alcohol is a poison.

For example, how many crimes have been committed under the influence of alcohol? How many deaths can be directly related to alcohol consumption? How many unwanted pregnancies? How many diseases? How many divorces? How many broken homes? How many fights? How many lost careers? How many tears? How many sorrows? The list of alcohol-generated tragedies is endless.

Yet, all this pain, suffering, sorrow, turmoil, and tragedy falls on deaf ears, blind minds, pleasure-seeking senses, money-based obsessions, and stone cold hearts. However, like the promoters of sex, the promoters of alcohol will ultimately be consumed by the very poison they hawk to the masses for their consumption. To recall the words of Saints Dariya and Ravidas respectively: *The sower of the poison cannot but be engulfed in the poison*, and *The fruit of action unfailingly overtakes the doer.*

Drugs

The consumption of drugs is, arguably, the most destructive destroyer of the S.A.D. ingredients and the most demonic PBO. If ever there were a satanic scourge in society, it is the usage of drugs. No sane person can argue against their negativity. But then again, how many sane people are there in this world? As Saint Dariya of Bihar remarked hundreds of years ago:

The world has indeed turned insane.

Drug usage is insidious and lethal. Peer pressure among young people prone to foolishness and social acceptance is often a deterrent to their highest and best good. This is another reason why we parents need to instill a strong sense of self in our children so they do not buckle under the pressures of their peers. After all, their peers will not take any responsibility for anything negative that happens to one of their "friends."

It is a fact that none of the proponents of S.A.D. will take any responsibility for anything untoward that happens to anyone following their advice or using their products and services. Life is all kisses, hugs, smiles, and parties when times are good, but when times turn bad the true character of such individuals shines like the sun at high noon on a cloudless day, as the perpetrators run away and hide, refusing to acknowledge their complicity with any untoward, negative, damaging, destructive, or lethal aspect of that which they promote, shamelessly.

As loving parents who desire the highest and best good for our children, we must educate them regarding the downside of each component of S.A.D. Certainly, no one pushing these poisons is going to talk about the nefarious, dangerous, and lethal consequences of such substances and their usage. They will be quite deceptive in their manipulations and ploys to get people to purchase and use their products and services.

This issue of pleasure-based opiates brings to bear a chilling quotation from Saint Charan Singh:

No matter how great the pleasures of the world may be, they are not only short-lived but also have equally unpleasant reactions at some time or another.

Translation: *great pleasure brings great pain.*

For all of those individuals engaged in promoting the Temptations of S.A.D., they would be well-served to also take to heart the following statement by Saint Jagat Singh:

The law of karma is universal. It is the fixed and immutable law of nature. Each soul must reap what it has sown. Every soul shall have to bear the exact consequences of its actions.

If you harm, injure, or destroy anyone or any thing, the same will be done to you to the same degree. It is just a matter of time. Whether in this life or beyond, you *will reap* the destruction, pain, sorrow, suffering, tragedy, turmoil, tumult, and tears you created, promoted, or supported. You cannot escape this reality, no matter what you believe.

Teaching Tips

1. Know the truth of S.A.D. and PBOs.

2. Be vigilant. Do not bury your head in the sand and pretend these poisons are unreal and cannot affect your family and loved ones.

3. Talk to your children. Educate them. Teach them the dark side of these poisons. Show them examples of people who have misused sex, drugs, and alcohol. Point out to them how their potential misuse and poor decision making can, and will, have a negative impact on their own lives.

4. Continually reinforce the potentially destructive nature of S.A.D. and PBOs. Don't delay. Your children's health, well-being, and future depend on positive parental guidance and involvement.

5. If we want to influence our children, teach them well, and protect them, what better way for us than being the living example of what we preach? Of course there is no better way, so in loving our children, sacrificing our questionable habits for their sake and ultimate success is obligatory. The famous doctor, humanitarian, theologian, philanthropist, and Nobel Peace Prize recipient Dr. Albert Schweitzer lucidly stated:

> *Example is not the main thing in influencing others. It is the only thing.*

What a great piece of advice, especially for parents!

The Two Sides Of Life

Day and night, male and female, yin and yang, up and down, in and out, north and south, east and west, hard and soft, hot and cold, heads and tails, joy and sorrow, smiles and frowns, tears and cheers, winners and losers, sickness and health, positive and negative, good and evil, love and hate, war and peace, life and death – these are just a few examples of the dual nature of this world. To be sure, there are two sides to everything. Understanding this fundamental principle of life will help our children better manage their lives from cradle to grave.

Why will understanding this universal principle of duality help our children? If we parents, from the get-go, raise our children to acknowledge and understand that there are two sides to everything in life, our children will be better equipped to return to a centerpoint when difficult and challenging times present themselves. As previously mentioned, *balance is primary*. Having knowledge of life's duplicity in all things will hopefully allow our children to stay on the balance beam and avoid a fall into an abyss.

For example, how many times have children encountered some problem or upset in their lives? The list is endless. Unfortunately, the negative aspects of such problems often get top billing with the children becoming totally absorbed, even overwhelmed with it all, especially with the negative side of the proverbial coin. However, every coin does have two sides. This is where wisdom enters and saves the day. When we parents can explain to our children that there is a light side to every dark side and to concentrate on the light side, then kids have some knowledge to help them better manage the negativity which they're allowing to affect and upset them.

And let's be clear. No one really can upset us. In truth, we allow others to upset us via our own lack of balance, strength, wholeness, and centeredness. When we have a strong concept of ourselves then nothing anyone says can possibly have any negative effect on us. This is why teaching our children to be strong, whole, self-realized, and independent is powerful – it keeps them centered and in a place (emotional, intellectual, spiritual) where few things in life can hurt them, especially low-level, ignorant, immature thoughts from low-level, ignorant, immature individuals.

There is negativity in this world. It will never go away. As Saint Sawan Singh states:

This world is a furnace in whose fires the soul is purified.

This truth is corroborated by Saint Charan Singh:

This world will always be at daggers drawn.

Therefore, teaching our children the truth of this "daggers-drawn" world and not allowing them to think or believe in the illusion that everything is wonderful and hunky-dory, will establish a sense of reality in them – a centerpoint from which to manage their lives more truthfully and efficiently.

On the other side of the Reality Coin, there is good in this world. There is love, decency, generosity, nobility, beauty, and positivity. We need to teach our children this as well. The point to be made is obvious – there are two sides to life, one positive and one negative; one light and one dark. We need to be aware of both sides if we're to lead and live a balanced, substantive life.

Where's the Blessing?

One of the most powerful antidotes to turn a negative experience into a positive affirmation of life is to ask the person beset with a severe challenge, *Where's the Blessing*? This may shock them at first, and hopefully it will do so in a positive way.

By asking *Where's the Blessing*? we reverse the flow of thought from negativity to positivity. We challenge the individual to see the other side of the coin, for as surely as there is a head, there is a tail; as surely as there is night, there is day; as certainly as there is a curse, there is a blessing. It is impossible for there not to be. No situation is totally dark and foreboding, totally negative. When our children are taught this simple skill and it becomes part of their consciousness, they will be better able to manage the downturns in their life's journey.

Up and Down

In considering the two sides of Nature's coin, we should never forget that life energies do not move only in one direction. If there is progress, there is also regress. If someone can climb, they can fall. What goes up can certainly come down.

Why mention this? Because when life is good and we are riding high on the crest of a fortuitous wave there is the possibility that we may forget the dual concept of life, subsequently making decisions and committing actions that are not in our best interest and which will create a fall.

For example, how many rich, famous, celebrated, and popular icons throughout history in all cultures have come crashing down in a fiery display of ignominious cataclysm? But why did they fall? A cursory assessment may well reveal that, frankly, they got too big for their britches. Their self-consumption overpowered their self-effacement. Their arrogance and false belief in their invulnerability was the fateful chink in their armor.

As we teach our children to manage the negative aspects of their lives by countering them with positive aspects, so we must also teach them to guard against falling from a high place. In other words, they must learn humility. If we allow our children to become too big for their britches, too consumed with their own egos, too self-absorbed at the expense of others, they could well be headed for a fiery crash of their own.

Nobody is so big that he or she is invulnerable to the laws of Nature, which always work to balance. Many individuals have, unfortunately, learned this the hard way. Let's do our best to make sure our children understand this so they can live a happy, fulfilled, and balanced life.

Teaching Tips

1. Make the children aware of the concept of two sides of life. Inculcate it in them through repetition and discussion.

2. Point out examples of where people were stricken with suffering but rebounded with an undying spirit of moving on and never being defeated. Likewise, share examples with your kids about those people whose egos overpowered their humility and crashed and burned as a result in disgrace and ignominy.

3. If you sense your children are getting too big for their britches, check them on it. If their egos get out of hand, they will be headed for a fall, and no parent wants that.

4. Teach children to *find the blessing* in each hurt. Bring them to a centerpoint of balance.

Where Have All The Manners Gone?

In the 1960s the American folk singing group Peter, Paul and Mary, popularized a Pete Seeger song entitled, *Where Have All The Flowers Gone*? It is not an unfair question in these early years of the 21st Century to ask, "Where have all the manners gone?"

What are manners? Manners are social modes of action expressing respect and deference for others. Manners, or the lack of them, speak to the character of an individual and a culture.

The famous German writer, artist and politician Johann Wolfgang von Goethe (18th/19th Centuries) stated:

> *A man's manners are a mirror in which he shows his portrait.*

In other words, an individual's social behavior and conduct reveal who he or she is at their core. Manners are an instant snapshot of a man's mindset and character.

There was a time when young people would automatically address their elders, teachers, employers, etc., as Mr., Mrs., Miss, Ms., Sir, or Ma'am. It was also common for young people to use the words "Please" and "Thank You" with regularity. Never would a young person talk back to a parent, teacher, employer, law enforcement officer, or authority figure.

Yet, this is not the general status of youthful behavior today. There exists a mindset of self-importance, entitlement, equality with adults, rudeness, and a lack of respect across the board with many young people.

Such a condition of mannerless behavior is unseemly, immature, and will not serve young people in the long run. Children are not adults. They have neither the experience, understanding, nor wisdom that only a life long-lived can create. Until they prove themselves and their worth, they are not entitled to place themselves on par with adults. Certainly they should not show them disrespect. In fact, when children are disrespectful to their elders, they are actually showing a disrespect for themselves and sowing the seeds for themselves being disrespected.

It is not incumbent for adults to show respect to children first. It is children who must demonstrate their respect and manners first to adults. Can a child provide for his own food, shelter, clothing, schooling, activities, etc., that parents provide? No. Children must be taught to recognize the sacrifices their parents and elders make for them and respect them for it. There is a natural hierarchy to life in which elders should be respected and given deference. Children may be the future, but it is elders who gave them the opportunity of a future. This alone demands respect and acknowledgment, which are encased in the social convention we call *manners*.

How did our youth get this way – mannerless and deprived of an understanding of how to interact with adults? Obviously, one reason is that they were not trained properly. Parents and adults did not insist on their children and young people being respectful. Another reason is that this age seems to be intrinsically inflicted with an infestation of crudeness and entitlement.

Richard Buckminster Fuller, 20th Century American futurist, author, inventor, and designer aptly noted:

> *Parents are usually more careful to bestow knowledge on their children rather than virtue, the art of speaking well rather than doing well; but their manners should be of the greatest concern.*

Buckminster Fuller's observation reflects the relationship between true success in life and simple worldly achievement. True success in life is based on an understanding of life, not merely on the ephemeral expression of fame, fortune, titles, celebrity, popularity, and placards on a wall. How life really works – this is what Buckminster Fuller is referencing, and it is a strong foundation in manners that keeps the foundation of society strong and in tact.

When we do not teach our children to have manners, we are hurting their potential for success because we are teaching them to ignore, devalue, discredit, even deprecate the natural order of life. This will not serve them well as they grow into their adulthood. Respect is critical to anyone's success in life, and if such respect is not made an integral part of children's characters their road ahead will not be smooth.

As a father, grandfather, and martial arts instructor I have always, and will always, demand those young people under my care learn and demonstrate respect for themselves and others. I don't know of any substantive martial arts instructor who feels differently. It's fine to be independent and free, but we all live in a social environment, and the social structure demands there be a certain level of respect and deference to others if society is to function smoothly and efficiently. Respect should certainly be given to those who have gone before us and shown the way, who have created a foundation on which we stand, who have given us opportunities we would not otherwise have had it not been for their sacrifices and hard work.

Furthermore, social rank and status are not the sole determiners garnering a show of manners from others. Respect is about acknowledgment, sans titles and certainly sans egos. An elderly person, for example, regardless of race, color, achievement, title, or gender deserves as much respect as a person who has achieved some semblance of worldly accomplishment. There are many, many people in this world who may not have the trappings of what is perceived as being successful but who are truly successful as far as life is concerned. Therefore, manners – and a good set of them – should be demonstrated to all people, especially one's elders.

Teaching Tips

1. Make manners an integral aspect of a child's character. Insist they use the words "Please" and "Thank You" as a natural part of daily living. After all, no one has to do anything for anyone. Have them reference other non-familial adults as Mr., Mrs., Sir, Miss, Ms., or Ma'am.

2. When introducing a new adult to your children, have the children extend their hand while looking the adult in the eyes. This not only shows respect, but it also creates a sense of confidence in the children because, by looking into someone's

eyes as you speak to them, it erases the fear of personal interaction. It's actually quite empowering. In my martial arts business I make every child introduce themselves to adults by shaking their hands and looking them in the eyes while standing upright and speaking clearly and distinctly. This method is empowering because it not only teaches self-confidence and self-assuredness but respect – all qualities that will help the children as they grow into their own adulthood.

3. One unusual but powerful strategy I use is to have my students choose their favorite teacher, approach them, extend their hand, look them in the eyes and say, "Good morning, Mr., Mrs., Ms, or Miss, how are you today?" This is a powerful strategy because it teaches young people to be proactive in establishing themselves as a strong individual who has a sense of respect and manners. In fact, I tell them to "Draw First," which means to extend their hand before anyone else. This makes them active, not reactive, and creates strength and character. How many children actually do this? Can you imagine the talk in the teacher's lounge? Such behavior immediately sets these children apart from the crowd, giving them a reputation that is deserving of respect and admiration, especially from adults and teachers.

4. Monitor your child's manners during social events. Never criticize children for having a lack of manners, but rather talk to them about the positive reasons for having manners, i.e., it shows respect, creates strength, develops confidence, and engenders the

good graces of others because it acknowledges them, and who is there who does not want or love to be acknowledged?

The bottom line is that when children demonstrate manners everyone wins. There are no downsides to having respect and deference for others.

Your Life, Your Responsibility

The world is getting weirder by the day, and one of the saddest and most problematic indications of such weirdness is the infestation in the mind of many people that someone else or some thing else is responsible for them and their welfare. People playing victim, pointing fingers, blaming others – it's all unnatural, unspiritual, unseemly, and destructive to the human spirit.

Infants, incapacitated individuals, and the failing elderly can legitimately look to someone else to assist them in their lives, but other than that, who would not want to take control of their own lives, be accountable, be strong, be noble, and have some dignity? Is comfort, ease of living, and enjoying life on someone else's honest work worth the sacrifice of one's character?

The reality of life is that this is our life and it is our responsibility. This is just a natural fact of life. There's no getting around it, there's no gray area, and any thought to the contrary is simply wrong and misguided.

To attempt to make others responsible for us is to admit we are helpless and can't take care of ourselves. By looking to others to take care of us says we still need a mommy, daddy, nanny, or government to help us survive. Where is the nobility of living by handouts, especially when we're able and capable of working and making our way in the world? Where is the dignity in looking to others to care for and be responsible for us? Is that really how we want to live? Really?

Here's a test question: if you somehow found yourself isolated and alone on a desert island, who would you look to for your care, welfare, shelter, food, clothing, etc.? There's only one answer, you. Period. So given such a reality, why do we look to others to support us? Are we weak? Have no backbone? No independent spirit? No courage? No grit? No fortitude?

What would those individuals who founded America say if they could see what much of America has become? No doubt they would turn over in their graves if they could see the state of many Americans today. Frankly, it's pitiful and sorrowful. When will those individuals who are not taking responsibility for their lives wake up and take control of their lives rather than abdicate their personal power to the power of others? Occasionally, as humans we all need help, but to make a lifestyle of depending on others for our continued well-being does not bode well for our character.

The message of my experience to every child is, has been, and will always be: *This is your life and it is your responsibility*. The short form is: *Your life, Your responsibility*. It's no one else's job to care for you. I told my kids the following . . .

> *As a parent, it's my job to care for you when you're growing up, but when you are an adult, it's your job to care for yourself, your children, your family. My job is to feed you, clothe you, house you, love you, support you. Your job is to do your best in school and create a foundation for your future because this is your life and it is your responsibility.*

Does this seem harsh? Not to me, and here's why. The only way we can protect our kids, whom we love dearly, is to make them strong, confident, self-reliant, courageous, and competent so they can take care of themselves. We actually weaken and cripple our children when we make life too easy for them. We enable their dependence rather than cultivate their independence when we do not raise them with the reality that this is their life and it is their responsibility.

This philosophy is no less the same for leaders of communities and countries. When leaders make decisions and laws to inordinately care for the people they lead, they weaken them, not strengthen them. Making people dependent is not the way to greatness in leaders, people, or nations. Great leaders edify and inspire the souls they serve, never weaken, cripple, or devalue them.

The natural extrapolation of dependence is subjugation and slavery. It is a gross dereliction of duty and responsibility for any leaders of a home, community, business, organization, or country to weaken those whom they serve. Exalted leadership demands exalted vision and exemplary action.

What happens when our children become adults? Will they be able to fend for themselves? Make their own way in the world? Survive? Will we have helped them grow strong, independent, courageous, self-reliant? Or will we have crippled them by neglecting to teach them that their life is their responsibility?

Of what value would any martial arts instructor have if he did not teach and train his students to defend themselves in a conflict? The reality of personal assault is that there is a likely chance that if you, for example, are ever attacked or assaulted, you will most likely be alone, and there will be no one there to take care of you or protect you except you. Then what? Psychological or emotional trauma? Maiming? Rape? Death?

In my women's self-defense workshops, I teach this acronym: Y.O.Y.O. It stands for *You're On Your Own*. The meaning of this is, as previously stated, if a person is attacked, especially a woman, she will most likely be alone, and therefore she will be on her own. If she was never taught to take care of herself but instead to look to others to protect and care for her, she may indeed live to regret it, if she lived at all.

In my martial arts profession I've seen the effects of rape and personal violation. Many women never recover from such an assault. It destroys them and, if they have families, there may very well be a negative effect on the children and husbands.

Here's the reality of life: if we don't take responsibility for ourselves, who's going to? The government? Friends? Family? Neighbors? Frankly, when we become adults no one in this world is responsible for us except us. We can spin the delusional fairytale that it's someone else's responsibility to take care of us but it won't change the truth. *This is our life and it is our responsibility.* Applied to our children when they become of age, *this is their life and it is their responsibility.* It is our duty as parents to help them grow into this irrefutable reality. This is how we protect them. This is how we love them. This is how we lead them – by teaching them the simple truth: *Your Life, Your Responsibility.*

Teaching Tips

1. Guide children by example. As parents, if we take responsibility for our lives, our children will most likely take responsibility for theirs. If they do not, then we must ask

ourselves where we failed. *The unexamined life is not worth living*, said Socrates, and as parents we would be well served to constantly examine our own lives, decisions, directives, and choices to assess whether we're being the best parents we can be.

2. Casually point out to children examples of how this person or that person is taking responsibility for their lives, decisions, choices, and how strong and powerful such actions make them. Let them know there is strength and nobility in taking charge of their lives and that allowing others to make choices for them weakens them, and, certainly, to blame someone else for their own actions, mistakes, or conduct is simply wrong and demeaning.

3. Directly, and often, remind children that *their life is their responsibility*. Do it lovingly, kindly, but do it. Don't neglect it. If this concept is not ingrained before the teen years, life will most likely be very challenging for them. In their developmental years have them fill in the blank to this statement: "Your life, your _____," or "Your _____, your _____." Then alter the line to "My life, my responsibility." When the teaching moment presents itself, you ask, "What is it?" The answer from them is, "My life, my responsibility." This is one of the most important principles our kids must learn while under our parental tutelage. If we neglect teaching them this fundamental concept of life, their lives and ours will be less than happy.

4. A few ways to teach personal responsibility are:

A. Have your children pick up their toys after they play. Ask them, "Are these your toys?" Of course they'll say "yes." Then you say, "Well, then, please pick them up and put them away. After all, they're your toys and you need to take care of them properly and put them away." Then see that they do it. Do not let them off the hook. Once they've put everything away, then give them some positive reinforcement.

B. When children make a mess, don't allow them to walk away without cleaning it up. "Whose mess is this?" you ask. When they respond in the affirmative, you say, "Your life, your responsibility. Your mess, your responsibility, right?" See that they clean up their mess. Do not do it for them. The sooner they learn to clean up their own messes, the better. If we do it for them, we enable their mess making, crippling and weakening them in the process.

C. Other things you can do are to have them make their bed every morning, clean their room once a week, take out the garbage, wash the dinner dishes, mow the lawn, trim the bushes, wash the car, pick up after the dogs, etc. – all activities that expand their consciousness to the reality that they are a part of their household and they, like everyone else, need to do their part to ensure a smooth, balanced, responsible life because, in the final analysis, it is their life and it most certainly is their responsibility.

You're On Your Own
Y.O.Y.O.

This principle, *You're On Your Own*, the acronym for which is Y.O.Y.O., was mentioned briefly in the section, *Your Life, Your Responsibility*.

It may seem somewhat harsh to teach our children that *you're on your own*, but it will be a great blessing for them as they grow to adulthood. Of course, when our children are under our care they're not on their own. They're in the process, if we do our job well, of learning to be self-sufficient, to be on their own because, eventually, they most certainly will be.

As adults, our children will have to stand on their own two feet, be counted as adults, not children, and be responsible for themselves. One of the ways we ensure this for them is to teach them this vital principle when they're young and in a protected, supportive environment.

In the second person, this principle of self-responsibility translates to *You're On Your Own*. In the first person it is *I'm On My Own*. It is this first person reality we must help our children internalize before they leave the warm confines of their home and step into a world that can often be very cold, cruel, callous, ruthless, deceitful, and wicked.

In the section *Your Life, Your Responsibility*, the analogy was given of a person being in a self-defense situation, the bottom line to which is that in such a case he or she will most likely be on his or her own. This is reality.

Even thinking that a friend who happens to be with us before an attack happens will be around *when* an assault occurs is unrealistic. It's sad but true that often when a person gets in trouble, others flee. It's like a horse getting spooked and taking off at a full gallop without any other thought but self-preservation – no care for his rider or other people standing around in his presence, even little children. If a horse is scared out of his wits, look out! Horses are prey animals with extremely well-developed nervous systems that are hard-wired to flee when threatened. In many ways people are the same.

Indeed, there are individuals who will stand by us when danger erupts, but history has proven too many times that such is not the case. It's a natural instinct for people to flee in the face of trouble while not thinking of anyone but themselves, just like horses. This is why those who do not flee but offer support and protection are known as heroes. They do not flee but think of others and, through courage and a sense of humanity, do what they can to help those in need.

One of the illusions of life we would do well as parents to make known to our children is that many of the people we think of as "friends" are not friends at all. This is true especially if we're successful, famous, rich, a celebrity, etc. – all things worshipped by the world. But just watch what happens when such magnetic accoutrements as fame, fortune, and celebrity go by the wayside or die out completely. Those people who professed to be "friends" will often flee in a flash, leaving you alone, stunned by their so-called "friendship" or rather lack of it.

This may be a harsh reality, but it is a sobering truth nonetheless. Saint Jagat Singh (20th Century) states:

> *Regarding worldly relationship, it may be pointed out that all relationships are based on selfish motives on this material plane. Husbands, brothers, wives, sisters, other relatives and friends are attached to us because of the advantages that accrue to them from us and are apt to cool down in their zeal and love towards us when they feel that we are of no use to them. Do not expect much from them but do your duty towards them and care for them even if they fail to reciprocate your love.*

By helping our children understand this truth of worldly relationships, they will remain balanced and centered when relationships fall apart or come to their natural conclusion. By being balanced and centered, they're more whole and therefore able to manage their lives more efficiently than they might otherwise be if they did not understand the truth of "friends."

This lesson was poignantly impressed upon me when my eleventh grade English teacher, Paul Benjamin, was found holding up five fingers to the class, moving his fully opened right hand from one side of the room to the other for what seemed like an interminable amount of time. He didn't say one word. He just kept moving that hand back and forth as he looked at us students. Finally after making an impression, which he did, he broke the silence and said:

> *If you have this many true friends in your life before you die, you'll be a fortunate individual.*

I can honestly say that since that day, and with far more than a full half century of life experience behind me, Mr. Benjamin was absolutely right. Yet, when we're young and idealistic we often cannot see, or refuse to see, the cold hard truths of life. Fortunately, Mr. Benjamin was one of those rare teachers who taught more than high school English.

If we allow our children to think that everyone who claims to be their "friend" is a friend, we will be doing them a disservice because we will not be educating them in the reality of life. For example, do our children actually think that their "friends" on Facebook and other social media websites are really their true friends? Are the relationships with such "friends" meaningful? Our kids need to be aware of who their actual friends are because when reality does hit, as it will, our children will not be as well-equipped to handle the situation as they would be if they had been given the truth of relationships.

Each of our destinies is different. Each of our children's destinies will be different. One child, for example, may have a destiny overflowing with an abundance of social energy, while another child may have a destiny of reclusion, withdrawal, solitude, and isolation.

We can actually know the blueprint of our children's destinies through their numerology charts (see *Parenting Wisdom for the 21st Century – Raising Your Children By Their Numbers To Achieve Their Highest Potential*). If, for example, a child has an abundance of 1-5-7 energy in his chart, the likelihood of him being alone in life is quite possible. In such a case, it would be extremely helpful to teach him the principle, *You're On Your Own*.

If a child's numerology chart maintains mostly social numbers (2-4-6-8), his life will be focused on relationships, the home, and socializing. In a way, this could be a trap because he may be fooled into thinking everyone's his friend but, as previously explained, friendship can be fickle.

Regardless of a child's destiny, it would behoove them to learn the reality of life – that ultimately *You're On Your Own*. In the final analysis, each of us must take responsibility for our own lives. This is a good thing, so let us not avoid it, and let us certainly not avoid teaching it to our children.

Teaching Tips

1. Let children do things by themselves. When they fall, don't rush to them. Let them figure out how to stand back up . . . on their own.

2. Give children chores to do around the house and allow them to do them on their own. Once again, don't offer help unless help is actually needed.

3. If a child of school age asks what a word means, have them research it on their own. Don't make it easy for them or for yourself. Make them do the work . . . on their own.

4. The message is pretty clear, right? The key phrase is *on their own*. Teach this concept early and often. It will pay dividends in the long run.

QUOTATIONS

Section	Quotation
A Divine Reality	*In the absence of any other proof, the thumb alone would convince me of God's existence.* ~ Isaac Newton
	God created everything by number, weight, and measure. ~ Isaac Newton
	It is the perfection of God's works that they are all done with the greatest simplicity. He is the God of order and not of confusion. ~ Isaac Newton
	Everyone who is seriously involved in the pursuit of science becomes convinced that a spirit is manifest in the laws of the Universe – a spirit vastly superior to that of man, and one in the face of which we, with our modest powers, must feel humble. ~ Albert Einstein
A Man's Worth Is Only Worth What His Word's Worth	*We must not promise what we ought not, lest we be called on to perform what we cannot.* ~ Abraham Lincoln

A Man's Worth Is Only Worth What His Word's Worth

Silver and gold are not the only coin; virtue too passes current all over the world. ~ Euripides

God looks at the clean hands, not the full ones. ~ Publilius Syrus

Balance Is Primary

You must tread your path with caution in the world. ~ Saint Dariya of Bihar

Man always travels along precipices. His truest obligation is to keep his balance. ~ Pope John Paul II

The best and safest thing is to keep a balance in your life, acknowledge the great powers around us and in us. If you can do that and live that way, you are really a wise man. ~ Euripides

Anyone can teeter-totter but not everyone can balance. ~ Anonymous

Be A Living Example

Example is not the main thing in influencing others. It is the only thing.
~ Dr. Albert Schweitzer

Be A Living Example   *Children always copy their parents.*
                                         ~ Saint Charan Singh

Better To Have A Gold Character Than A Gold Medal   *The first essential step to a spiritual life is character. One may deceive one's friends, relatives, and even oneself but the Power within is not deceived.*
                                         ~ Saint Sawan Singh

Only a man's character is the real criterion of worth.
                                         ~ Eleanor Roosevelt

Recommend to your children virtue; that alone can make them happy, not gold.   *~ Beethoven*

There was never yet a truly great man that was not at the same time truly virtuous.   *~ Benjamin Franklin*

Silver and gold are not the only coin; virtue too passes current all over the world.   *~ Euripides*

Of all the fragrances . . . the fragrance of virtue is the sweetest.   *~ Buddha*

Better To Have A Gold Character Than A Gold Medal

The superior man thinks always of virtue; the common man thinks of comfort. ~ Confucius

Few men have virtue to withstand the highest bidder. ~ George Washington

The only reward of virtue is virtue.
~ Ralph Waldo Emerson

Glory follows virtue as if it were its shadow. ~ Cicero

Character cannot be developed in ease and quiet. Only through experience of trial and suffering can the soul be strengthened, ambition inspired, and success achieved. ~ Helen Keller

The first prerequisite of a gentleman or a lady is a good moral character.
~ Saint Charan Singh

First Comes Ticker

Power tends to corrupt, and absolute power corrupts absolutely. Great men are almost always bad men.
~ Lord Acton

Give 'Em A Spine

Do what you feel in your heart to be right – for you'll be criticized anyway. You'll be damned if you do, and damned if you don't. ~ Eleanor Roosevelt

You have enemies? Good. That means you've stood up for something, sometime in your life.
~ Winston Churchill

Courage is what it takes to stand up and speak; courage is also what it takes to sit down and listen.
~ Winston Churchill

If you just set out to be liked, you would be prepared to compromise on anything at any time, and you would achieve nothing. ~ Margaret Thatcher

You may have to fight a battle more than once to win it.
~ Margaret Thatcher

We could never learn to be brave and patient if there were only joy in the world. ~ Helen Keller

Give 'Em A Spine	*Character cannot be developed in ease and quiet. Only through experience of trial and suffering can the soul be strengthened, ambition inspired, and success achieved.* ~ Helen Keller
Grown Ups, Own Up	*I blame not another, I blame my own karmas. Whatever I sowed, so did I reap. Why then put the blame on others?* ~ Guru Nanak
	What thou hast not done will never befall thee; only what thou hast done will befall thee. ~ Saint Dadu Dayal
High Bar, High Life Low Bar, Low Life	*The superior man thinks always of virtue; the common man thinks of comfort.* ~ Confucius
	Without recognizing the ordinances of Heaven, it is impossible to be a superior man. ~ Confucius
	The highest destiny of the individual is to serve rather than to rule. ~ Dr. Albert Einstein

High Bar, High Life
Low Bar, Low Life

Try not to become a man of success but rather to become a man of value.
~ Dr. Albert Einstein

Not everything that can be counted counts, and not everything that counts can be counted. ~ Dr. Albert Einstein

There was never yet a truly great man that was not at the same time truly virtuous. ~ Benjamin Franklin

Only a virtuous people are capable of freedom. ~ Benjamin Franklin

Nothing in our times has become so unattractive as virtue.
~ Edward Dahlberg

The wicked look on virtue with contempt for sinning is to them so great a pleasure. ~ Saint Kabir

It is the greatest good for an individual to discuss virtue every day . . . for the unexamined life is not worth living.
~ Socrates

High Bar, High Life
Low Bar, Low Life

No good deed goes unpunished.
                      ~ Clare Booth Luce

Be good and you will be lonely.
                      ~ Mark Twain

Heaven is being perfect.
                      ~ Richard Bach

The gull sees farthest who flies highest.
                      ~ Richard Bach

Do you have any idea how many lives we must have gone through before we even got the first idea that there is more to life than eating or fighting, or power in the Flock? A thousand lives, Jon, ten thousand! And then another hundred lives until we began to learn that there is such a thing as perfection, and another hundred again to get the idea that our purpose for living is to find that perfection and show it forth.
                      ~ Richard Bach

High Bar, High Life Low Bar, Low Life	*And when Abram was ninety years old and nine, the Lord appeared to Abram, and said unto him, I am the Almighty God; walk before me, and be thou perfect.* ~ Bible: Genesis 17:1
	Be ye therefore perfect, even as your Father which is in heaven is perfect. ~ Bible: St. Matthew 5:48
	Be as perfect as your Creator. ~ Saint Jagat Singh
	Ridicule is generally made use of to laugh men out of virtue and good sense by attacking everything praiseworthy in human life. ~ Joseph Addison
It's Not All About Them	*The world is a house of collyrium (an abode of evil), a veritable well of the poison of egotism.* ~ Saint Ravidas
Living With Grace	*Existence is suffering.* ~ Buddha
	This world is a field of suffering. ~ Saint Ravidas

Living With Grace

This world is the plane of struggle.
~ Saint Sawan Singh

The ideal man bears the accidents of life with dignity and grace, making the best of circumstances. ~ Aristotle

We should give as we would receive, cheerfully, quickly, and without hesitation; for there is no grace in a benefit that sticks to the fingers.
~ Seneca

Grace is but glory begun, and glory is but grace perfected.
~ Jonathan Edwards

Managing Opposition

Kites rise highest against the wind, not with it. ~ Winston Churchill

Courage is rightly esteemed the first of human qualities . . . because it is the quality which guarantees all others.
~ Winston Churchill

Destiny commands. We must obey!
~ Winston Churchill

Managing Opposition	*There has to be evil so that good can prove its purity above it.* ~ Buddha
	Out of suffering have emerged the strongest souls; the most massive characters are seared with scars. ~ Khalil Gibran
	And the trouble is, if you don't risk anything, you risk even more. ~ Erica Jong
	Our present life is already determined before we are born. What destiny has planned for you will come to pass without any planning on your part. Your destiny will cause you to act and make effort according to its plan. ~ Saint Jagat Singh
	Whatever is happening is all preordained. ~ Saint Sawan Singh
No Second Chance Guarantee	*For of all sad words of tongue or pen, the saddest are these, it might have been.* ~ John Greenleaf Whittier

No Second Chance Guarantee

I will prepare and some day my chance will come.
~ Abraham Lincoln

It is not often that a man can make opportunities for himself. But he can put himself in such shape that when or if the opportunities come he is ready.
~ Theodore Roosevelt

My country owes me nothing. It gave me, as it gives every boy and girl, a chance. It gave me schooling, independence of action, opportunity for service and honor.
~ Herbert Hoover

Unfortunately, there seems to be far more opportunity out there than ability. . . . We should remember that good fortune often happens when opportunity meets with preparation.
~ Thomas Edison

How much I missed, simply because I was afraid of missing it.
~ Paulo Coelho

No Whining	*Keep your mouth shut and suffer all in silence.* ~ Saint Kabir
Pity-Pot Poison	*I never saw a wild thing sorry for itself. A small bird will drop frozen dead from a bough without ever having felt sorry for itself.* ~ D. H. Lawrence
	Self-pity is our worst enemy and if we yield to it, we can never do anything wise in this world. ~ Helen Keller
	Never feel self-pity, the most destructive emotion there is. How awful to be caught up in the terrible squirrel cage of self. ~ Millicent Fenwick
The Five Needs of Children	*No man is free who cannot control himself.* ~ Pythagoras
The Two Sides of Life	*This world is a furnace in whose fires the soul is purified.* ~ Saint Sawan Singh
	This world will always be at daggers drawn. ~ Saint Charan Singh

The Temptations of S.A.D.

The affliction of lust is the foremost trap of the world. ~ Saint Ravidas

Sex indulgence is the lowest of human activities. That men should be at all proud of it surpasses understanding. ~ Saint Kabir

The sower of the poison cannot but be engulfed in the poison. ~ Saint Dariya of Bihar

The fruit of action unfailing overtakes the doer. ~ Saint Ravidas

If we kill we will be killed. We should never forget that. ~ Saint Charan Singh

The world has, indeed, turned insane. ~ Saint Dariya of Bihar

No matter how great the pleasures of the world may be, they are not only short-lived but also have equally unpleasant reactions at some time or another. ~ Saint Charan Singh

The Temptations of S.A.D.	*The law of karma is universal. It is the fixed and immutable law of nature. Each soul must reap what it has sown. Every soul shall have to bear the exact consequences of its actions.* ~ Saint Jagat Singh
	Example is not the main thing in influencing others. It is the only thing. ~ Dr. Albert Schweitzer
Where Have All The Manners Gone?	*A man's manners are a mirror in which he shows his portrait.* ~ Johann Wolfgang von Goethe
	Parents are usually more careful to bestow knowledge on their children rather than virtue, the art of speaking well rather than doing well; but their manners should be of the greatest concern. ~ Richard Buckminster Fuller
Your Life, Your Responsibility	*The unexamined life is not worth living.* ~ Socrates

You're On Your Own

Regarding worldly relationship, it may be pointed out that all relationships are based on selfish motives on this material plane. Husbands, brothers, wives, sisters, other relatives and friends are attached to us because of the advantages that accrue to them from us and are apt to cool down in their zeal and love towards us when they feel that we are of no use to them. Do not expect much from them but do your duty towards them and care for them even if they fail to reciprocate your love. ~ Saint Jagat Singh

If you have this many true friends in your life before you die, you'll be a fortunate individual.

~ Paul Benjamin

Note: "This many" equates to five fingers.

INDEX

Topic	Pages
Abraham Lincoln	19, 68, 111, 187, 198
AIDS	116
Albert Einstein	13, 80, 187, 192, 193, 216
Albert Schweitzer	27, 162, 188, 201
Alice Carey	84
Aristotle	22, 98, 196
Beethoven	32, 189
Benjamin Franklin	32, 80, 189, 193
Bible	83, 195
Bishop Mandell Creighton	66
Buddha	32, 82, 97, 112, 189, 195, 197
Capstone	149, 150
Chinese Tao	22, 24
Cicero	33, 190
Clare Booth Luce	81, 194
Confucius	33, 79, 190, 192
D. H. Lawrence	125, 199
Doctrine of the Mean	22
Edward Dahlberg	80, 193
Eleanor Roosevelt	32, 69, 189
Erica Jong	113, 197
Euripides	19, 22, 32, 188, 189
Franklin Delano Roosevelt	32
George Washington	33, 190
Golden Mean	22
Guru Nanak	75, 192, 210

Helen Keller	33, 71, 125, 190, 191, 192, 199
Herbert Hoover	117, 198
Iron Lady	70 (see Margaret Thatcher)
Isaac Newton	13, 187
Johann Wolfgang von Goethe	169, 201
John Greenleaf Whittier	117, 197
Jonathan Edwards	99, 196
Jonathan Livingston Seagull	82
Joseph Addison	84, 195
Khalil Gibran	112, 197
Lord Acton	66, 190
Lucius Annaeus Seneca	98
Margaret Thatcher	70, 191
Mark Twain	81, 194
Millicent Fenwick	125, 199
Nicolaus Copernicus	91
Paul Benjamin	183, 202
Paulo Coelho	118, 198
PBOs	155, 156, 161, 162
Peter, Paul and Mary	169
Pope John Paul II	22, 188
Publilius Syrus	19, 188
Pythagoras	141, 199, 215
Ralph Waldo Emerson	33, 190
Reality Coin	164
Richard Bach	82, 194
Richard Buckminster Fuller	171, 201
S.A.D.	155, 159, 160, 161, 162, 200, 201
Saint Charan Singh	28, 34, 158, 160, 164, 189, 190, 199, 200

Saint Dadu Dayal	75, 192
Saint Dariya of Bihar	21, 157, 159, 188, 200
Saint Jagat Singh	83, 113, 161, 182, 195, 197, 201, 202
Saint Kabir	81, 119, 156, 199, 200
Saint Ravidas	91, 97, 156, 157, 195, 200
Saint Sawan Singh	31, 97, 113, 164, 189, 196, 197, 199
Seneca	98, 196
Simon Says	105-106
Sir John Dalberg-Acton	66
Social Collective	121, 122, 123
Socialistic age	121
Socrates	81, 178, 201
STDs	157
St. Matthew	83, 195
Superior Man	19, 33, 79, 190, 192
The Confucian Analects	79
Theodore Roosevelt	117, 198
Thomas Edison	118, 198
Winston Churchill	69, 112, 113, 191, 196
Y.O.Y.O.	177, 181

Richard Andrew King
~ Books ~
www.RichardKing.net

The King's Book of Numerology
Volume 1 - Foundations & Fundamentals

The King's Book of Numerology, Volume 1-Foundations & Fundamentals provides complete descriptions of Basic Numbers, Double Numbers, Purifier Numbers, Master Numbers, the Letters in Simple and Specific form as well as the Basic Matrix, the numerological blueprint of our lives.

~

"*The King's Book of Numerology* series contains new information that informs and predicts more completely and accurately than any previously published numerological work. It brings back the empowered sciences of long ago, information long since lost upon this plane." ~ G. Shaver

"The best numerology book I've ever read." ~ M.W.

"I've learned as much about numerology from *The King's Book of Numerology* the last few days than I have in my past five years of study." ~ Frank M.

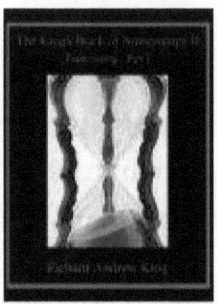

The King's Book of Numerology II
Forecasting - Part 1

The King's Book of Numerology II: Forecasting - Part 1 is dedicated to opening the door to the divine blueprint of our lives. That plan, that divine blueprint of destiny, is exact, precise, unchangeable, unalterable and . . . knowable, at least in general terms.

Once this awareness of a predetermined fate becomes established through application of numbers and their truths, our understanding and consciousness of life will, no doubt, change. We will begin to see ourselves as part of an immense spiritual super-structure far beyond our current ability to comprehend, understand or perceive. Life will take on new meaning and, perhaps, we will even begin to awaken to greater spiritual truths.

Subjects covered: Life Cycle Patterns, The Pinnacle/Challenge Matrix, Epoch Timeline, Voids, Case Studies and much more.

Blueprint of a Princess
Diana Frances Spencer - Queen of Hearts

The tragic death of Princess Diana of Wales - the most famous, the most photographed, the most written about woman of the modern world and possibly of all time - was one of the most shocking and saddening events of the late Twentieth Century. Not since the assassination of American President John Fitzgerald Kennedy in 1963, has such an event captured the attention of the world. On that ill-fated Sunday of 31 August 1997 and the following week until her funeral, there was much discussion and reflection of the Queen of Hearts, the People's Princess, England's Rose. But in all of the media news coverage, there was no discussion given to the cosmic aspects of her life and death. This book is dedicated to addressing those issues through The King's Numerology^{tm}. Its purpose and hope is to offer some consolation and explanation as to that one question so poignantly written on a card of condolence left with the multitude of flowers before the gates of Buckingham Palace. . . "Why?"

~

After learning from King's numerological teaching, it is impossible to conceive of going back to that 'twilight naive and foggy' state of being where one can only guess or hint at the truths, motivations and directions of one's life that are Pre-King. Not only do I recommend this book, but I suggest it and King's other numerology books as absolutely necessary for the library of anyone even remotely interested in the science of numerology. ~Hunter Stowers

Messages from the Masters
Timeless Truths for Spiritual Seekers

In a time where there is more need for enlightenment than ever before, *Messages from the Masters: Timeless Truths for Spiritual Seekers* offers timeless truths for genuine seekers thirsty for spiritual nectar.

Masters are the Ph.D.s of the universe, the Light Bearers of the Divine Flame. Their knowledge and wisdom are supreme. They have no equal. Although appearing human, they are not. Masters are the exalted Sons of God. Their chief duty is to rescue souls, liberating them from the maniacal maelstrom and madness of the material world and returning them to their eternal Home with the Lord.

Messages from the Masters is a rich source of hundreds of quotes from a cavalcade of nine Perfect Saints throughout the last six hundred years: Guru Ravidas, Kabir, Guru Nanak, Tulsi Sahib, Swami Ji Maharaj, Baba Jaimal Singh, Sawan Singh, Jagat Singh and Charan Singh. The messages in this book focus on the importance of the Divine Diet, the priceless Human Form, Reincarnation, the World, the Negative Power and Soul Food.

Warning! *Messages from the Masters* is not for the faint of heart or the worldly-minded. Masters come into the world to sever our attachment to it, not make it a paradise. Although the epitome of love and wisdom, they shoot straight from the hip, pull no punches, favor no religion. Their universal message of soul liberation is reflected in the statement of Saint Maharaj Charan Singh: *Just live in the creation and get out of it!*

99 Poems of the Spirit

99 Poems of the Spirit draws from the writings of Perfect Saints, Masters, Mystics and Sacred Scriptures. Designed to lift the consciousness, mind and heart, all of the poems are original works by Richard Andrew King. Their purpose is to help connect the reader with the mystic side of life in order to enhance the process of self-realization while advancing on the spiritual path and climbing the ladder leading to the ultimate attainment of God Realization. It is a treasure chest of poetic spiritual gems offered to excite, educate and stimulate the mind and soul in the glorious journey of spiritual ascent.

A few selected poem titles are:

A Thousand Mile Journey
Animal Food
Awake, Dear Soul
Between Two Worlds
Cards of Life
Child of the Light
City of the Dead
Glittering Lights
Karma
King of Fools
Lady of the Light
Reaping Weeping
Serious Business
The Wheel
We Reap the Deeds
World of Fools

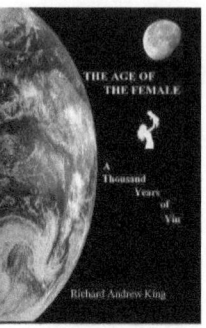

The Age of the Female
A Thousand Years of Yin

The Age of the Female: A Thousand Years of Yin highlights the profound and extraordinary ascent of the female in the modern world, placing her center stage in the global spotlight as presidents and leaders of nations, titans of industry, corporate executives, military generals, media magnets, doctors, lawyers and a whole host of other prestigious titles normally associated with the male.

Why has her rise to prominence been so rapid, especially in consideration of historic time? Why also has there been an increased interest in other people's lives in our society, in competitive athletics, personal data collection and the exploration of space and other worlds?

The Age of the Female: A Thousand Years of Yin answers these questions. It is an insightful and exciting read into these mysteries, offering compelling and irrefutable evidence through the ancient science and art of numerology that, indeed, the age of the female has arrived and the next thousand years belong, not to him, but to her.

The Age of the Female II
Heroines of the Shift

The Age of the Female II: Heroines of the Shift continues the remarkable journey of the female's ascent in the modern world of the 2nd Millennium.

This installment is a general read in five chapters honoring the accomplishments of women in categories of female firsts, female Nobel laureates, female athletes, female icons and female quotations.

The achievements of the women featured in *The Age of the Female II: Heroines of the Shift* are deserving of respect and admiration. Their lives, challenges and successes are motivational catalysts for every individual to be the best he or she can be and to honor the very essence of what it is to be human.

The Age of the Female II: Heroines of the Shift is intended to be an inspiring and educational read for everyone, not just women but men, too, offering knowledge and insight of the depth, power and daring-do of women as their Yin energy rises upon the global stage in this millennium which destiny has irrefutably marked as the Age of the Female.

The Black Belt Book of Life
Secrets of a Martial Arts Master

The mystery and mystique of the martial arts is not only ages old, it's legend. Revered throughout the world, martial arts is a treasure chest of life secrets that transcend the boundaries of combat to include the expanse of life and living. Arguably, martial arts is a great system for teaching the integration of body, mind and spirit.

The Black Belt Book of Life: Secrets of a Martial Arts Master is not about physical fighting strategies and tactics. It is about concepts and principles we learn though martial arts training that can help us in the struggle of life and in the journey to conquer ourselves. In the end, a true Black Belt should be a realized soul who, having engaged the enemy – himself – finds himself, triumphant.

The Black Belt Book of Life: Secrets of a Martial Arts Master reveals many secrets of martial arts training, sharing these truths in quick and easy to read vignettes to benefit martial artists and the general public as well. It is a book for all readers, not just martial artists, both males and females, especially the youth of today who are in search of a foundation to guide their lives.

www.KingsKarate.net

Your Love Numbers
Discovering the Secrets of Your Life, Loves and Relationships

Your Love Numbers reveals the secret formula defining all great relationships and how to assess the love potential of any relationship.

Your Love Numbers reveals the mystery of love through the most ancient of all sciences . . . numbers, your numbers, calculated using only your full name and date of birth and those of the people you love! "Numbers rule the universe; everything is arranged according to number and mathematical shape," said Pythagoras. And, yes, everything, including love, can be measured in numbers!

Your Love Numbers is based on research by master numerologist, Richard Andrew King. Applying his unique and revolutionary new theories, love and attraction between people can be determined using very easy to learn concepts. With a little study and practice, all this can be done in a matter of minutes.

Your Love Numbers teaches you how to assess a relationship or potential relationship in minutes, saving you endless time, energy, effort and possible heartache in the end. By knowing ourselves and the people we love, our relationships will be potentially more rewarding, satisfying, productive, peaceful, lasting and loving . . . for everyone - our family, spouses, partners, children, friends.

www.YourLoveNumbers.com

Destinies of the Rich & Famous
The Secret Numbers of Extraordinary Lives

Why are rich and famous people rich and famous? Is it luck? Hard work? Advantage by family name? What makes them special? What secrets are the basis of their success?

- Why is Oprah Winfrey a billionaire entrepreneur?
- What gives Sarah Palin her Going Rogue persona?
- What caused Marilyn Monroe to be a sex goddess?
- What caused Princess Diana's tragic life and death?
- Why was Michael Jackson plagued by child issues?
- Why was Howard Hughes a disturbed, rich recluse?

Destinies of the Rich & Famous explores the secret numbers of the following famous global icons and explains through The King's Numerologytm why they are both rich and famous.

Dr. Albert Einstein	Marilyn Monroe
Amelia Earhart	Michael Jackson
Elvis Presley	Muhammad Ali
General George Patton	Oprah Winfrey
Howard Hughes	Princess Diana
John F. Kennedy	Sarah Palin

www.DestiniesOfTheRichAndFamous.com

Parenting Wisdom for the 21st Century
Raising Your Children By Their Numbers To Achieve Their Highest Potential

This book is a must for any parent and all parents to be. It is vital to read this book now before you name your children. If you already have children, then it is just as important to understand them. Richard Andrew King should be called Dr. King. His books are of the magnitude that will be read with reverence for generations to come. ~ Dr. Victoria Ford, J.D.

Parenting Wisdom for the 21st Century - Raising Your Children by Their Numbers to Achieve Their Highest Potential is a revolutionary addition to the process of arguably the most important job in the world, parenting.

Master Numerologist, father and grandfather Richard Andrew King teaches you the secrets to understanding your children's destinies through the most ancient of all sciences, numbers.

The powerful information contained within this work will reveal the hidden desires driving your children, the paths they will follow in life, the roles they will give on the great life stage and much more – all designed to augment your parenting wisdom and support life's paramount parental purpose . . . to love the children and help them achieve their highest potential.

www.ParentingWisdom.net

To order books, go to
www.RichardKing.Net
and major online booksellers

Contact

Richard Andrew King

PO Box 3621

Laguna Hills, CA 92654

www.RichardKing.Net

Email: Rich@RichardKing.net

www.ingramcontent.com/pod-product-compliance
Lightning Source LLC
Chambersburg PA
CBHW030232170426
43201CB00006B/193